CONTEMPORARY ART & POP.

First published 2002 by order of the
Tate Trustees distributed for
Tate Liverpool by Tate Publishing,
a division of Tate Enterprises Ltd,
Millbank, London SW1P 4RG
www.tate.org.uk

The moral rights of the authors
have been asserted.

British Library Cataloguing in Publication
Data. A catalogue record for this book is
available from the British Library

ISBN 1 85437 425 7

Distributed in North and South America
by Harry N. Abrams, Inc., New York,
under the following ISBN
0-8109-6265-9

Library of Congress Cataloging
in Publication Data
Library of Congress Control Number:
2002104373

This book has been
published to accompany the exhibition:
Remix: Contemporary Art and Pop
Curated by Simon Wallis
Supported by
The Liverpool Culture Company Limited
Organised by Tate Liverpool
25 May – 26 August 2002

Designed by
Big Corporate Disco, London

Reproductions by
Lazertype, Wrexham

Printed by
St Ives Multimedia, Blackburn

The editors would like to thank
the following Tate Liverpool staff for
their contribution to this catalogue:
Jemima Pyne, Claire Young,
Catherine Sadler, Julie Robson and
Helen Stalker.

Tate Liverpool would like to thank the
following organisations for their support

/ Liverpool is known the world over for
its pop music heritage, pre-eminently
through The Beatles, but also through bands
such as Echo and the Bunnymen, Teardrop
Explodes, Frankie Goes to Hollywood,
OMD, China Crisis, The La's, Boo Radleys,
Cast, Atomic Kitten, Ladytron and The Coral.
Historically, because it was the first point
of entry for American soul and pop records,
it became a centre for appreciation of
pop music with a strong dance culture from
late 1950s. The popularity of dance
and club culture in the city speaks of a
continuing creative tradition which
Remix: Contemporary Art and Pop uses
to draw emotive analogies between the
world of contemporary art and that of
popular music in all its manifestations.
/

/ The DJ technique of remixing has been
used since the mid 1960s when King Tubby
and Lee Perry first started to experiment
with dub music in Kingston, Jamaica. The
fusing and reconfiguring of a wide range
of influences is at the heart of our sampling
culture and *Remix* explores this eclectic
and pragmatic spirit where chronologies are
shuffled and new connections are made.
In *Remix*, pop music and art history are
a resource to be plundered and the works
in this exhibition reflect a pick and mix
DJ mentality that comprises nostalgia, irony
and connoisseurship. This way of thinking
has long been at the centre of popular
music, including deconstructive homages
to Broadway show tunes in the jazz of
John Coltrane and Miles Davis; the
mood-shifting psychedelia of The Beatles
and Pink Floyd; the mixing and sampling
used by Grandmaster Flash, Afrika
Bambaataa and De La Soul; or the fully
sampled soundscapes of The Avalanches,
DJ Shadow or Ritchie Hawtin, to name only
a handful.
/

/ *Remix* features artists who use the
imagery, spirit and techniques of pop.
For these artists music is a form of inspiration
and their work – from the 1990s through
to the present day – reflects the visual
cultures of film, video and photography
that are closely associated with the
appreciation and consumption of pop.
They examine and exploit musical histories,
the desire to idolise pop stars, DJs and
groups, the glamour of celebrities, the
impulse to perform, as well as crowd
behaviour at concerts and in club culture.
I would like to thank Simon Wallis, curator
of *Remix*, for once again sharing his great
sensibility for topical trends in contemporary
art, for his careful selection of artists and
works and his intelligent catalogue essay.
/

/ Our thanks go, above all, to the artists
for their enthusiasm and hard work.
We are also extremely grateful to all the
lenders who have generously supported
the exhibition by allowing us to borrow
their works.
/

/ We are especially grateful for the
generous support of this exhibition by
The Liverpool Culture Company Limited.
Remix brings together the creative traditions
of music and art that have played such
an important role in this city for more
than half a century. The exhibition continues
this vital tradition into the present and
the future, supporting Liverpool's bid for
European Capital of Culture in 2008.
/

/ Tate Liverpool is most grateful for the
sponsorship of *Remix* by Masterfoods, a
division of Mars UK Ltd. We also
acknowledge the support granted to us by
Music Mall, London and The Australia
Council for the Arts. We also thank Big
Corporate Disco for their innovative
catalogue design.

Christoph Grunenberg
Director
Tate Liverpool

Our sincere thanks go the following
for their invaluable help in organising
the exhibition –

* Irene Bradbury and Sophie Greig
at White Cube, London
* Jenny Blyth
at The Saatchi Gallery, London
* Molly Dent-Brocklehurst
at Gagosian Gallery, London
* Walter Cassidy and Brian Doyle
at 303 Gallery, New York
* Corinna Durland
at Gavin Brown's enterprise, New York
* Carol Greene and Molly McIver
at Greene Naftali, New York
* Alison Jacques
at Asprey Jacques, London
* Elly Ketsea and Rosa Bacile
at Lisson Gallery, London
* Darren Knight
at Darren Knight Gallery, Sydney
* Gregorio Magnani
at Magnani, London
* Dale McFarland
at Frith Street Gallery, London
* Sara Meltzer Gallery, New York
* Philip Nelson
at Galerie Nelson, Paris
* Maureen Paley and James Lavender
at Interim Art, London
* Laura Ricketts
at Anthony d'Offay Gallery, London
* Andrew Sielewicz
at Victoria Miro Gallery, London
* John Tevis
at Goldman Tevis, Los Angeles
* Andrew Wheatley
at Cabinet Gallery, London

CONTENTS

POP:
THE SOUNDTRACK TO OUR LIVES

BY SIMON WALLIS

Each of us has a personal soundtrack to our life, as music helps to construct memories by amplifying emotions and moods. We use pop music as a form of escapism to be imaginatively, and often nostalgically, taken elsewhere. Pop is rooted in the contingencies of time and place, and each moment of history since the 1950s has had its own soundtrack – either the most played single or album, or the most talked about group or artist. Thinking back over the 1990s any list of pop names associated with that decade conjures up a wide variety of memories and associations: Primal Scream, Oasis, Blur, Massive Attack, Tricky, Portishead, Beck, The Verve, Aphex Twin, Goldie, Supergrass, St. Etienne, Radiohead, The Beastie Boys, Robbie Williams, The Spice Girls, TLC, Take That, Madonna, Mary J Blige, Missy Elliot. All of this is, of course, highly contingent and each of us can add our own favourites as we think back to where we were, what we were doing and with whom we were doing it. Many contemporary visual artists use this associative and emotive power of pop music as an element in their work. The artists in *Remix* exploit the immediacy of pop as well as its more subtle aspects, which engage with desire, aspiration and the construction of taste.
/
POP
NOSTALGIA
/ It's revealing to consider which aspects of pop music history remain pertinent to each generation. One has only to look at the current appropriation of 1970s progressive rock, early punk, psychedelia and 1980s electro pop to begin to make diverse connections across the decades. There are still untold numbers of contemporary bands and musicians linking their music firmly to that of other eras, which, seen from a historical distance, are often evoked as more authentic moments for culture. The 1960s pop of The Beatles, The Beach Boys, The Velvet Underground, The Kinks and The

Rolling Stones remains seminal in our current music vocabulary. The 1970s gave us Roxy Music, The Ramones, The Sex Pistols, Public Image Limited and Joy Division, who are still pop touchstones for many young acts. Similarly, the 1980s electro pop of Kraftwerk, The Human League, Gary Numan and Soft Cell has influenced a whole generation of black American musicians to create electro, house, techno and hip hop, and continues to be recycled into new genres. Hybridisation has been the name of the game in the best forms of pop for the last forty years. New sampling technologies have pushed this tendency forward to enable ever more complex bricolages of sound, which define a new aural landscape using musical history as a resource.
The sense of nostalgia that pop employs cyclically is developed by some of the artists in *Remix*, who look back to celebrate the past as well as ponder its future uses.
/
TECHNOLOGY
AND
IMPROVISATION
/ New technology encourages innovation and improvisation in attempts to stay ahead of the pack and avoid obvious musical clichés. Complex time signatures are

created and airtight sounding samples played off against one another. Many musicians have moved away from the orthodoxy of guitar-based bands to embrace a closer relation to technology and the gadget culture that amplifies the power of the body. The dialogue between art and science comes to pragmatic fruition through musician-engineers who work in recording studios to create new music where the quality of sound becomes crucial. Paradoxically, this music is made with scientific precision to derange our senses and engage our passions.
/
/ It's only those of us who grew up without computers, colour television, digital television channels, video recorders, the internet, email, CD players or mobile phones, that feel the pace and quality of change over the last decade. Those now in their teens, and younger, are entering a radically altered culture from that of the 1970s and early 80s, particularly as the internet has helped fuel an explosion of genres for every conceivable interest group. Consequently, the autonomy of the once fabled modernist art object has been shattered by what it feared most: theatricality, contingency and sensual pleasure. Dance and pop music are

perfect examples of this process as they fracture and mutate into diverse categories at an extraordinary pace. These genres continue to develop in different western cities, particularly New York, Chicago, London, Los Angeles, Detroit, Dusseldorf, Bristol and Sheffield, allowing local culture to tailor what it needs to satisfy an audience. This diversity is technologically driven as new software is learnt, enabling the creation of previously unimagined soundscapes.
/

/ It was the binding of music and visual culture through concerts, clubs and 'happenings' in the 1960s that laid the foundation for the type of connections that the artists in *Remix* wish to make. Contemporary technological culture embodies the 'expanded mind' that so many proponents of the supposed benefits of LSD were espousing in the 60s. Technology allows us to access and expand our world without having to alter our brain chemistry – not that it stops anyone from still wishing to do so. The 60s gave us a legacy of strategies for breaking down hierarchies as Pop art began to pilfer and play with the dominant commercial culture. Artists could now look much further afield for subject matter and were not afraid to open up their work to the everyday facts of popular and media-generated imagery. The DJ techniques of scratching and sampling, which became standard forms of pop practice from the late 1970s, extended this, offering new ways for using pre-existing material. Post-punk bands started to engage with many different forms of music and developed groundbreaking dialogues with black American dance music and Jamaican reggae. In the 1980s and 90s new technology became cheaper, making it easier to create and manipulate hybridised music without the need for an expensive studio in which to record. These developments made pop and contemporary art a vital part of the

changing face of DIY culture that has become intensively mediated and saturated with new products and genres.
/

THE
DJ
PARADIGM

/ All the artists in *Remix* use, consciously or not, the paradigm of the DJ, who reconstructs music and choreographs performances at clubs, gigs and on the radio. The DJ is one of the key figures in building a new aesthetic for the twenty-first century and has a mandate to recombine and loosen musical boundaries. The successful DJ has an immense knowledge of music built from enthusiasm and driven by the fast technological pace of changing styles and audience responses. Many DJs add to this by recording as artists under a simultaneous roster of different names, each specific to the type of music being made. The DJ creates these new forms to redefine chronologies and experiences while never losing sight of human desire manifested in love, sex, dance, melody, rhythm and song – which are the essential components of pop. The DJ has enabled us to become ever more subtle and attentive in listening to and experiencing music, as the 'turntablist'

mentality is highly pragmatic and sensual. The DJ uses what works, which is easily measured through audience reaction. He or she uses the history of recorded music as a resource to create remixed amalgamations that define emerging genres.
/

/ Many of the artists in *Remix* have an eclectic sense of reinterpreting history because they do not necessarily buy into the idea of immutable structures and can enjoy and use 'a look' and 'a sound' as much as 'a position'. Art and pop history is for these artists a living personal thing that can be recycled and reused, not merely catalogued and coolly dissected by those who closely guard their idea of a canon. This generation of artists is too busy taking in a wide array of influences to worry about how to make it all correspond to any hierarchical and theoretical stance that would merely close options down. Uniqueness may now be privileged in the connections that can be made rather than as a paradigm that eulogises the isolated genius and the 'authentic' gesture. Remixing becomes a way of layering stories and interests, reconciling disparate elements in creating new experiences from our rich pop culture.

REMIXORAMA

PT01 — PUFF DADDY

PT02 — MIXMASTER MORRIS

PT03 — COLDCUT MIX

BY CEDAR LEWISOHN

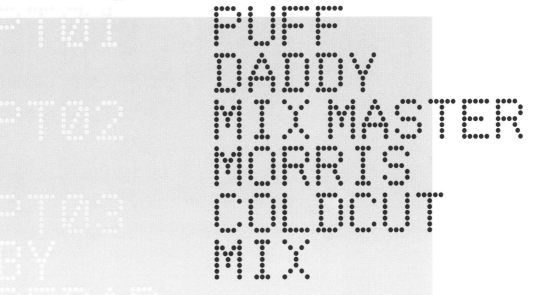

PART
01
PUFF
DADDY

The living legend: Sean Combs. His approach to music fits well with an explanation or complement to this whole *Remix* project. And spun right, there might be a chance of a great scoop. Not only has he based an entire career on appropriation and remixing, but the choice of songs to rap over is so…inspired. Also, because everyone has heard of him, no introduction is needed. For Satoshi Yamzaki, Puff Daddy was not only the living embodiment of remix, but the very pinnacle of hipness. Everyone's been remixed by Puff, and those who haven't, are in line. He's even remixed his own name. PD to P Diddy.
/
/ And Diddy's style of sampling was so much more blatant. He didn't take loops, he took the whole song, sang over it, released it, made mo' money. Hip hop karaoke-ist. Boom shakka, no doubt. But when PD rapped over Sting's *Every Breath You Take*, it was so much more than a cover version, more a manifesto. The words and melody stayed the same but the song was given a new immoral sensibility. Heartbroken power pop to pop-hop murder ballad. Few could deny the brilliance of this homage to murdered rap star Notorious B.I.G. (another of Satoshi's heroes). It had all the qualities and characteristics needed to define remix, but rendered in a shrewd, cheeky, and mainstream way. You have to hand it to Didd: even back in the day his ish was slick. By employing such heavily loaded source material and subverting the frame of reference, Puffy in effect used pop's own hand to give itself a firm slap in the face.
/
/ Anyway, and more to the point, Satoshi imagined Puff would be great to interview, like some egomaniac preacher dressed in white fur and gold chains, waxing lyrical about the inspiration for his new triple

platinum LP and the number of helicopter explosions in the video. She wanted in on the BLING BLING glitz. Unfortunately PR in New York weren't eating it. They were cagey and suspicious from the jump-off. PR wanted a list of questions and to know where Puffy's portrait was gonna be hung in the exhibition. What network would the interview premiere on? PR laid it on the line: 'Mr Combs is a spiritual man who's deeply interested in the arts. Mr Combs likes the Tate Gallery. His schedule however doesn't allow for interviews to no-fee productions with audience ratings below the five million mark.' On the upside PR could provide promotional merchandise for the duration of the show, seeing as the UK is a charity an' all.
/
/ Unfortunately Satoshi had made the clumsy mistake of being honest. The response was unsympathetic. After trying to explain that Tate Liverpool weren't proposing to exhibit a portrait of Puff, and Fruity TV, a small indie film company, were making a documentary on the subject from which the exhibition had taken its name, communications simply dried up. So Satoshi was left on a mission into remix, without guidance from her would-be mainman, PD.

```
WHAT'S              OUT
INTERESTING         CÉZANNE
IS                  FROM
THIS                THE
IDEA                TUBE.
OF                  YOU'RE
PEOPLE              SQUEEZING
USING               OUT
AS                  SOMETHING
THEIR               THAT
MATERIALS           ALREADY
THINGS              HAS
THAT                LOADS
ARE                 OF
NOT                 CULTURAL
NEUTRAL.            RESONANCE
MORE                IN
AND                 IT.
MORE,
ARTISTS             BRIAN
ARE                 ENO
WORKING
WITH
MATERIALS
THAT
ARE
ALREADY
CULTURALLY
CHARGED.
THAT'S
DIFFERENT
FROM,
SAY,
SQUEEZING
OUT
CADMIUM
RED
FROM
THE
TUBE:
WHAT
YOU'RE
DOING
IS
SQUEEZING
```

'A remix is something that comes out and still has the original artist's name on it... plus the remixer's. That's different from a sample,' states the Mix Master kind of blunt.
/
/ 'Totally,' agrees Satoshi, 'samples is selected cultural reference points for audience, or maybe audience don't recognise.'
/
/ 'Definitely. Using samples is to do with playing with the recognition factor. But if the audience recognise it, the lawyers recognise it too,' laughs Morris then continues, 'the hardest thing is to remix something that's brilliant to start with. I mean Coldcut are doing a remix of *Rockit* by Herbie Hancock. I don't envy them.' Adapts voice to something like a game show host...*'because it's got to be better...or what's the point?'* Laughs.
/
/ 'Yeah...classics is most difficult subject to remix.'
/
/ 'I heard they're remixing the video too. Did you ever see that?'
/
/ Satoshi looks blank.
/
/ 'It was a landmark. From the days when MTV said they wouldn't play any video with a black person in it.' S gives a cutesy smile, MMM continues, 'so Herbie Hancock made a video with dancing robots instead. The only time his face appears he's on a TV in the corner of the room. MTV were like, 'yeah, yeah OK, it's got a nigga in it, but he's so small no one's gonna know.'
/
/ Both laugh. Satoshi awkwardly, then interested. 'How many times did that all last?'
/
/ 'Errr...until Michael Jackson, I think.

Billie Jean was the first black music video to get on MTV.'
/
/ 'Hmmm...' ponders Satoshi, skimming her notes.
/
/ 'Famously.' Morris finishes his sentence. Then offers, 'I'd better not tell you the Michael Jackson story.'
/
/ 'Oh...*come on*,' begs S.
/
/ 'OK,' he agrees, easily persuaded. 'Tell the camera guy to turn that thing off.'
/
/ They're back on.
/
/ 'Kind of like remixing his face,' laughs Satoshi. Then stumbling out some words skew-whiff, 'if...is our...er...if, if our idea of remix entwined...'. Annoyed at her English, she changes question: 'some people make remix albums, but haven't released their own music album and they got very famous, do you think so?'
/
/ 'Yeah, that's been a major trend in the last five years,' concurs Morris. Then at a slight tangent, 'ten years ago, it was *we don't know how anything works. We want someone to remix us.'* Nowadays you get mixes by bands – the Manic Street Preachers mix or whatever. It's because computer skills are more readily available, people aren't intimidated by the equipment.'
/
/ Camera guy's panning the room. Walls lined from floor to ceiling with filed and categorised vinyl. S and MMM in front of two PC monitors that hum and distort through the viewfinder. Beneath the screens, anonymous but expensive looking samplers and effects boxes are stacked. Anoccasional tiny red or blue bulb flash from the equipment giving the room the

PART B2
MIXMASTER
MORRIS

feel of an airplane cabin or spaceship. Shelves of CDs and walls plastered with gig posters from raves and clubs around the world, all bearing the handle Mix Master Morris. The door and ceiling are covered with holographic wallpaper, its repeating circular pattern dancing in the light. The camera zooms into a photo of techno legend Derrick May holding a copy of Morris' *Flying High* album.

/

/ Swinging back onto the pair of them, Satoshi asks, 'where's future for remix?'

/

/ Exhaling spliff smoke as he speaks, MMM chuffs, 'the term is becoming looser and looser because everybody wants in on it. So nowadays most people have grown up with the idea that one song comes in multiple forms.'

/

/ 'Then how do I recognise good stuff?'

/

/ 'Hmm…now you're asking. A good remix is one that makes the music better than it was before. Something that completely turns one thing into another and makes you listen to the original differently.'

/

/ 'It's more than music idea though, hah?,' comes more squeaky Nipponese English.

/

/ 'I don't think so. It's important not to confuse remixing and cultural expropriation.'

/

/ Not what Satoshi wanted to hear. So as any good journalist would, she asks the question again, using different words. 'What about multiple personalities. Kind of like image remix?'

/

/ MMM's not having it however. 'Nah, Madonna reinventing herself every year doesn't count, nor does a pseudonym on the internet. Because it's one person

creating another version of how they see themselves. In terms of sex, that would be masturbation. For a lot of people it's very unethical to remix yourself. Why remix yourself? Can't you decide how you want your own music to sound? Remixes should supply something more unpredictable, something more anachronistic.' Despite this 'incorrect' response, Satoshi's feeling confident (the new Burberry shirt perhaps?) and she explains in some detail her Sean Combs theory before enquiring, 'you like Puff Daddy?'

/

/ 'Not really,' says Morris flatly. 'Puffy's just A & R isn't he? Always has been. Pure Tin Pan Alley. Which is why the industry loves him and cool people hide their heads under the blankets to avoid it. He's got a Pete Waterman heart beating in there.'

/

/ Satoshi looks on in a mild state of disbelief…outrage building fast…fury thermometer turning from beige to red. But she remains poised, even professional, holding her ground with, 'but his interpretation of songs, it's very bold, you must admit he's pioneering?'

/

/ 'You mean instead of making his own tracks to rap over he takes an MOR hit from the 80s and raps over that. It's unbelievably tacky,' replies Morris, oblivious to Satoshi's smouldering venom. The camera doesn't pick it up either, only a sweet Japanese hip hop kid saying, 'thank you very much Mr Mix Master Morris. We got what we need from you.'

THE
CONCEPTUAL
FRAMEWORK
FOR
THIS
REMIX
IDEA
WAS
ESTABLISHED
IN
THE
FIRST
TWENTY
YEARS
OF
THE
TWENTIETH
CENTURY.
IT'S
A
RESPONSE
TO
TECHNOLOGY
AND
THE
ADVENT
OF
RECORDING.
IN
LITERATURE,
PEOPLE
SUCH
AS
TRISTAN
TZARA
PRODUCED
WORK
THAT
CAN
BE
SEEN
AS
REMIXING
EXISTING
TEXT.

MARCEL
DUCHAMP
USED
OTHER
PEOPLE'S
WORK
TO
MAKE
HIS
ART.
ERIK
SATIE'S
MUSIC
D'
AMEUBLEMENT
WAS
MADE
FROM
FRAGMENTS
OF
ALREADY
EXISTING
MUSIC.
THESE
ARE
EARLY
EXAMPLES
OF
REMIXING
AND
SAMPLING.

DAVID
TOOP

95% of the yoot walking around today have never even heard of Marilyn Monroe. Definitely not seen *Diamonds Are A Girl's Best Friend*. Marilyn Manson however, they like. So when you get Manson (that's Marilyn, not, er…Charlie) singing Eurythmics' *Sweet Dreams (Are Made Of This)*, there's a fair bit of layered referencing going on or 'cultural expropriation', as MMM put it. All this reminded Satoshi of postmodernism, endless narratives and the death of the original. Which put her in a head spin until the next afternoon when she and the film crew found themselves in the kitchen of one half of dance music pioneers Coldcut.
/

/ The decor of Matt Black's kitchen had that '91-Summer-of-Love-techno-hippie-vibe going on. Yin and Yang signs, Hindu suns and such, plus kids playing on a laptop. The scene opens with Satoshi and Matt jiving for a time. Coldcut produced *Say Kids*, the UK's first sample-based hit and the seminal 1987 remix of *Paid in Full*. Satoshi and Matt discuss the lack of green – only £700 for something that sold a few million units worldwide and went on to define a genre. The lo-tech production, no samplers, just recorded live off decks. Eric B and Rakim's (the original artists) vexed reaction to the mix. The *Top of the Pops* incident with Rakim attempting to mime to a song that had the rap vocals replaced with sound bites from old movies and cartoons. Matt makes the point that these records introduced the idea that you could put all sorts of unexpected material down over a dance groove and still keep people's interest – even expand the range of what they're prepared to listen to. The interesting comparison for Satoshi is that with innovative music, just as with innovative artworks, the protagonists further the expectations of what the audience perceives as acceptable within a specific context. Be that gallery or dance floor.

Then she asks for Matt's definition of remix. Which he articulates thus: 'To most people remix would be something to do with dance music and getting a DJ to produce a new version of a record. Basically, it's a sampling collage that you get paid for making. It's a job.'
/

/ 'So can remix word work outside music?'
/

/ Gesturing to the prep notes which he'd read earlier, Matt replies 'well in those, you talk about the deconstructive homages to Broadway show tunes and the music of John Coltrane and Miles Davis. That's already expanding the remit of the term beyond what most people would understand.' In her mind ideas are taking wing, the reassuring nature of revivals, safeness in familiarity and the luxury of choosing which information to choose from. The thoughts are brain-filed for later as she asks, 'where does remix combine visual culture?'
/

/ 'Well I mean literally, we, as Coldcut, have commissioned visual remixes. We've had a video that we've made,and given it to someone to remix. That's not being done all that much, but I'd expect it to take off as an interest in DIY visuals develops. Modelled on the way DIY sound construction took off.'
/

/ So relieved to hear this, after the trouble yesterday with that Mix Master Morris dude's bad attitude. Satoshi is upbeat 'I have theory, like think of Andy Warhol as visual remixer. Maybe Marilyn Monroe is a beat, or sounds, that loop and repeat. Little bit like techno music…'
/

/ 'I think there's two things there,' says Matt, before sneezing. 'There's Warhol taking Marilyn Monroe's face, and sort of putting an effect on it, as one would

PART
03

COLDCUT
MIX

add an effect to an existing beat or sample. Then there's the aspect of repetition, which is a separate thing.'
/
'Right, yeah,' is the quick response.
/
/ The action lingers on Matt who stares at Satoshi for a second: she's wearing a blue crop top bearing the words MOTOR CITY BABY. Her dyed blonde hair is up in bobbles and she's got black plastic chains round her neck. Matt's feeling flu-ey, but phases back into the conversation with 'in dance music, where the term remix comes from, repetition of elements has become very important. And it's, er…the human brain likes patterns, and pattern recognition. It's designed for it.'
/
/ Slightly lost here but wanting to keep things flowing, Satoshi gives another 'right, yeah.'
/
/ MB continues with the science: 'so we like patterns…and a rhythm is an audio pattern that we latch on to and identify. If there's no variation within that pattern, once you've sussed it, you get bored. Music and visual arts tread a thin line between establishing the pattern and putting enough variation in there so it doesn't become boring.'
/
/ 'I'm with you 100%' she lies, and changes the subject. 'But why is sampling so linked with dance music and hip hop?'
/
/ 'Well, partly because in the evolution, that was coded in.'
/
/ 'Evolution?'
/
/ 'In the evolution of music to form where we are now. When hip hop started in the late 70s, you had Kool DJ Herc with two turntables, getting two copies of the same record so he could play the bit people really liked continuously. That's credited

as the first real time vinyl remix.'
/
/ 'That's big' smiles Satoshi, truly amazed.
/
/ 'It was really before the term 'remix' existed, except maybe in some of the New York discos. But there he was, remixing. It wasn't long before people moved on from using two copies of the same record to mixing in whatever they felt like, which was a massive inspiration for us as Coldcut.'
/
/ 'OK, last question. Remix first listed into English dictionary in year 1989, has meaning changed since then?'
/
/ Camera focuses on Matt.
He sneezes again, then states, 'remix is now a widespread term with some use in culture, which I accept. But I'm not sure it means anything more than the reggae concept of 'version', which predates it, and is perhaps more useful, because when you do a remix, you're really making a version or interpretation of someone else's work.'
/
/ 'Wicked,' chimes Satoshi, wrapping things up.
/
/ After saying their thank yous and goodbyes, the crew rounds up the kit, and takes a few establishing shots of the house's exterior. Our heroine sits and waits in the people carrier, chewing on a Bubblicious and planning the voice-over for her film. Something about remix as a form of schizophrenic mutation and the remixed product as a fragmented double. She may pose the question: 'if remix is a result of reality deceased, does that mean in the postmodern epoch we inhabit, only the fake survive?' But she may not. Another thing she plans on mentioning is that remix as a concept is now officially over twenty years old (some would say over eighty),

yet it still has a fledgling freshness that every sound wants a piece of, from garage to classical. And that remixes can be a cynical marketing tool used by record companies to target niche markets. It has the power to give the most mainstream pop act a touch of avant-garde respectability, at the same time allowing exposure for esoteric mavericks.
/
/ She imagines a lengthy roving opening shot of the exhibition installation with her voice-over explaining how remix and sample culture provide the comforting reassurances of the popular past, with the added bonus of allowing its participants the opportunity to appreciate what they may have missed first or second time round. With Biggy Smalls blaring through the speakers of the Renault Espace, Satoshi gazes at a mini crucifix hanging above the dashboard. Remix is like European Jesus she fancies, resurrecting the dead and offering eternal life to the mundane or forgotten. But also, and perhaps more importantly, remixing can deliver miracles, equivalent to turning the essential, like water, into the celestial, like wine.

REMIX :

WARHOL, HAMILTON, ENO, WOLFE: FOUR WAYS OF LOOKING AT ART AND POP.

BY MICHAEL BRACEWELL

'The cast was a new, younger, post-Pop group of kids (like Jane Forth, a sixteen year old beauty with great shaved eyebrows and Wesson-oiled hair). All the morality and restrictions that the early superstars had rebelled against seemed so far away – as unreal as the Victorian era seems to everybody today. Pop wasn't an issue or an option for this new wave: it was all they'd ever known.' *Popism: The Warhol Sixties* Andy Warhol and Pat Hackett (1980)

/ You could make the case that Pop (and let's make Pop a proper noun, following Warhol's lead that Pop is a tangible thing, as much as a state of mind) has become for contemporary artists what landscape and portraiture were for painters of the eighteenth and nineteenth centuries. And this is largely because Andy Warhol was right in every detail about the direction of the consumer Zeitgeist. His book *The Philosophy of Andy Warhol*, published in 1975, now reads like prophecy: today,

we're surrounded by Pop in a mass media culture which is fuelled by celebrity, from the triumph of 'Pop Idol' in the TV democracy, to Madonna handing out the Turner Prize on live television, and using the occasion to advertise her new album.

/ To Warhol, Pop was the totality of popular culture, of which popular music was simply a strand. And the same is true today for contemporary artists, to whom pop music as a subject – its rituals, stars and rhetoric – is usually a refinement of the wider world of total Pop. This wider world doubles as a generational rite of passage, bending Pop to self-portraiture, through appropriations of fan base folk art, or serving as a means of subjective anthropology through which to make social comment.

/ In many ways, the relationship between Pop and art has always been one which answers to the notion of the 'remix'. There is a fluidity of connections between the two media, and an ability for one to sample from the other. If we follow the line that Pop in the contemporary sense can be dated from the release in the UK of Elvis Presley's *Heartbreak Hotel*, back in the spring of 1956, then we can also follow a parallel line – pretty much immediately – of the impact of Pop on the visual arts. For here was a whole new subject, and, one could argue, a whole new problem for contemporary artists. If total Pop was a manifestation of the modern world, then what might be its dialogue with art? A few of the answers to this immediate question would become classic numbers in their own right, and demand repeating because they remain equally valid today, because Pop was always going to be a transatlantic thing, in terms of both vinyl and philosophy.

/ The great British actor Malcolm McDowell – who starred in the triptych of seminal Pop movies of the late 1960s and early 1970s

If.., O Lucky Man! and *A Clockwork Orange* – recollected that his father's hotel in Liverpool boasted not only the longest bar in the north-west, but that its clientele of sailors brought with them the latest of American pop music, in the same way that American airmen once had, over at the Burtonwood airbase. McDowell also recounted riding the bus to Lime Street, and seeing the 'bright red electric guitars hanging up in the shop window'. He added, 'you knew you could never afford one, but they gave you hope somehow'.

/ With regard to the import of Pop ideas in relation to art, it was Warhol who seemed to have the first and last words in the early 1960s, prior to the emergence of Liverpool and London as the reigning hot spots of total Pop, for a while at least, as Detroit, New York and the West Coast cities of America began to get their mythologies in place. For Warhol, driving across America to California with Taylor Mead, in October 1963, his identification of Pop – which was pretty much every aspect of modern consumer culture that he saw on the sides of the roads – was also a revelation of speed: a short-cut to the future ('Pop Idol' and Madonna presenting the Turner Prize here we come!) achieved by Pop awareness.

/ Warhol recounts his discovery in *Popism*, through the transcription of his impressions into a literary form by his diarist Pat Hackett. And the observation stands as one of those founding insights into the relationship of the remix between Pop and art that we touched on earlier. On recognizing Pop as the new art Warhol says:

/ 'The moment you label something, you take a step – I mean, you can never go back to seeing it unlabelled. We were seeing the future and we knew it for sure. We saw people walking around in it without knowing it, because they were still thinking in the past, in the references of the past. But all you had to do was know you were in the future, and that's what put you there.'

/ In contemporary art, Warhol's pronouncement of knowing the future can be felt in the work of an essentially documentarist artist such as Rineke Dijkstra. Her video clips of clubbers at Liverpool's Buzz Club and Mysteryworld in Zaandam – once you consider them in the light of Warhol's equation between labelling and the future – can take on a science fiction aspect. Twitching or staring, vagued out or wary, these young people in Dijkstra's video (punning on Warhol's *Screen Tests*, perhaps, only now the kids aren't

auditioning for anything, not being on planet Pop Idol but one of its lesser moons) are the direct descendants, the living proof, of Warhol's pronouncement on the post-Pop group of kids for whom Pop would never be 'an issue or an option... It was all they'd ever known.'

/ This question of speed and time seems central to the relation between Pop and art. The historian and Sex Pistols' biographer, Jon Savage, makes the distinction in 'Speed', the final section of *Time Travel*, his selected essays 1977–1996. Savage identifies speed as the core element in the development of Pop as both iconography, lived experience and music – the power surge on the circuitry between Elvis and Pere Ubu's *Thirty Seconds Over Tokyo*. In his introduction to *Time Travel*, Savage writes:

/ 'Speed is vital because it is one of the few areas where teens are more powerful than adults, and time has been frequently used to express a rebellious attitude. You need think only of Sly Stone exquisitely cocking a snook at the world in the lyrics of *In Time* – Kairos as Staggerlee. In Punk classics like *The Last Time* and *No Time*, The Rolling Stones and The Saints may well be directing their comments – as immature men are prone to do – at individual women, but the message is in the insolent drones of the music: a direct challenge to the established order, whether it's the nursery demons of the music industry, or authority figures like parents, teachers and politicians. I'm faster than you: I'm five years ahead of my time.'

/ Savage's subsequent extrapolation of Pop's speed into a loop (illustrated by The Beatles' *Tomorrow Never Knows*, as a record marking the conversion of Pop time from linear to circular) raises issues for contemporary artists who identify in Pop the slowing down or acceleration of memory –

the timescale of memoir – and, most important, the distinction made by Michael A Collins, in *The Likes of Us: The Official Biography of the Working Class*, between history and nostalgia. This is explored in Mark Leckey's extraordinary video montage *Fiorucci Made Me Hardcore*, showing clubbers on the Northern club circuit from Northern Soul of the 1970s through to rave in the 1980s and 90s. In this work we experience a slippage between history, nostalgia and what feels like the lux cinema of the mind – memory itself, or a collective memory in which figures and scenes become poeticised by time's acceleration or slow motion.

/ The footage of an agile young male dancer from the 1970s, or of young women living out the rituals of weekend partying, brings to mind not only tracks such as the Pet Shop Boys' *Saturday Night Forever* or The Human League's *Sound of the Crowd*, but also the novelist Jeff Noon's observation that 'dance music is essentially melancholy'. (Pop's melancholy, perhaps, is Savage's speed of youth, only seen as elegy, as youth must always age: 'Spring-heeled Jim feels the chill,' sang Morrissey, 'Oh, where did all the time go?')

/ With regard to the classic, founding philosophies of Pop, Andy Warhol's Pop–triggered time travel to the future (described by the artist in 1963) was of course precursed in the UK by Richard Hamilton's definition of pop art from 1957. It's a list well worth repeating, as it remains as valid a description of Pop as it did forty-five years ago. One could apply, in fact, all of Hamilton's terms – his list of Pop's ingredients – to the creation of the Spice Girls or 'Pop Idol'.

/

/ 'Pop art is: [wrote Hamilton]
Popular (designed for a mass audience)
Transient (short term solution)
Expendable (easily forgotten)
Low cost
Mass produced
Young (aimed at youth)
Witty
Sexy
Gimmicky
Glamorous
Big Business.'

/

/ Between 1957 and the present day, the boundaries between art and Pop have become blurred on countless occasions, but the fundamental distinction between the two – Pop and art – remains as obvious as the difference between a sunset and a painting of a sunset: however fused in sensibility, or translated by the art-making process, the signifier and the signified remain firmly separate. In this much, the source material of pop art – that organic

totality of popular culture, doing its own thing in the Zeitgeist – is possessed of an independence which art reflects in the 'remix': Pop lends its iconography to an act of creative translation, out of which may emerge further icons.

/

/ Richard Hamilton's definition of pop art, therefore, could be said to find a contemporary articulation in Gavin Turk's effigy of himself, entitled *Pop*, as Sid Vicious in the Elvis pose transcribed from a cheesy Hollywood western by Warhol. Here is Popism in concentrated form: Turk's sculpture passes through six pop loops (Elvis, Hollywood, Warhol, Vicious, *Rock 'n' Roll Swindle*, Turk) to update Hamilton by way of the Sex Pistols, with Turk himself attempting a self-portraiture which is at once heroic and mock heroic – a bad boy's bedroom shrine to a real punk rocker, and a chunk of postmodern Irony for the twisted denim generation.

/

/ In the early 1960s, Pop and pop art found a co-existence in the fact that The Beatles themselves were described by Hamilton's definition of the form, as well a whole iconography of Pop which shuttled between commerce and culture. You could think of the Union Jack fabric developed by Geoff Reeve at the Royal College of Art in 1965, which would provide the suiting for John Entwhistle of The Who's famous 'Union Jacket'. From this we pass into the Pop Union Jack imagery that became ubiquitous (reaching critical mass in the *Time* magazine

cover of April 15 1966, 'London, Swinging City'): from the paintings of Derek Boshier to the sunglasses sold at Gear boutique on Carnaby Street.

/

/ It is this aspect of Pop, the 'artisan' aspect, working within the totality of popular culture, which Tom Wolfe, the great American novelist and cultural commentator, finds investigative of the broader role of pop art. For Wolfe, the artisans working within popular culture are of more interest as artists than the art stars who borrow from their work. Wolfe is concerned throughout his writing with the anthropology of the modern world according to status, and one can find in his analysis (leaving aside his personal judgements of worth) an insightful view of a particular form of contemporary pop art – the fan base folk art paintings of Elizabeth Peyton, Gary Hume and Dawn Mellor, for example, or the sampling videos of Candice Breitz.

/

/ In the equation of remix between Pop and art, Tom Wolfe's distinction between the artist and the artisan is of crucial importance, however intolerant of contemporary cultural practice it might appear. In an essay published in the catalogue for the *Los Angeles Environment* exhibition, held at the Los Angeles County Museum of Art in 1976, entitled 'Chester Gould versus Roy Lichtenstein', Wolfe delivered the exact counter-argument to Warhol's acknowledgement of Pop labelling – what Warhol saw as the alchemical process of re-labelling between popular culture and art, Wolfe refutes as little more than piracy:

/

/ 'Once a visual phenomenon is categorized as part of popular culture, this is a signal to everyone in the art world that it is not necessary to take it seriously, although one is perfectly free to enjoy it in the spirit of Camp or nostalgia for the mud. This was precisely the spirit of Pop art. Warhol, Lichtenstein, Oldenburg, Indiana and the rest brought back comic strip panels, Campbell's soup cans, Brillo boxes, Rexall drug store boys' first basemen's mitts and neon signs in the spirit of anthropologists returning with tribal masks. They were capturing for the world of high culture the icons created by energetic but unsophisticated and nameless artisans who did commercial design for the populace...out there. It was on this point, however – namely, sophistication – that Pop art ran into problems.'

/ In his earlier book, *The Painted Word* (1975) about the development of contemporary art from abstract expressionism through Pop to minimalism (in which he argues the case for a literary quality within art itself), Wolfe describes the conversion of popular commercial art source material (he hates the term 'popular culture') into Pop art as being related to the status of perception. For Wolfe, pop products created outside of the art world are regarded by those in it as being deliciously kitsch or Camp, but habilitated into big art money seriousness by being described by the leading critics as 'signage'.

/ This is directly relevant to the practice of contemporary artists dealing with Pop: very often there is a mixture (as we see in Turk's *Pop*) of two parts Camp and Irony

to one part celebratory homage. This is also the case in those artists who riff on faux-naif fan base folk art, or the cheesy allure of mainstream pop. In a bravura passage from *The Painted Word* – 'Hello Steinberg' – which remains controversial today, Wolfe writes:

/ 'In short the culturati were secretly enjoying the realism! – plain old bourgeois mass-culture high-school goober-squeezing whitehead hunting can-I-pop-it-for-you-Billy realism! They looked at a Roy Lichtenstein blow-up of a love-comic panel showing a young blond couple with their lips parted in the moment before a profound, tongue-probing, post-teen, American soul kiss, plus the legend 'We rose up slowly...as if we didn't belong to the outside world any longer...like swimmers in a shadowy dream...who didn't need to breathe ...' and – to hell with the sign systems – they just loved the dopey campy picture of these two vapid blond sex buds having their love-comic romance bigger than life, six feet by eight feet, in fact, up on the walls in an art gallery. Dopey...campy...'.

/ Wolfe's identification of the 'dopey campy' allure of Pop for artists is a further founding philosophy in the remix between the two forms. It can be seen to blow the whistle on a certain sleight of hand when it comes to the status games of perceptive intent, and it holds its truth for the post-Hirst generation of artists for whom the very idea of 'Dopey Campy' is central to their practice. This is the

art based on Pop which serves as a comedy of recognition (but seldom, interestingly, a comedy of anxiety) within the rites of passage: the dopey campy aspect of Pop as a soundtrack to growing up – a romance, in fact.

/ Jon Savage notes that Roxy Music's first hit, *Virginia Plain*, is a Richard Hamilton painting brought to life, so the fact that Bryan Ferry – one of the co-founders of Roxy Music, along with Brian Eno, Andrew Mackay and Phil Manzanera – was tutored in Fine Art at Newcastle University by Hamilton himself, provides a neat historical circularity. More than any other group since The Velvet Underground, Roxy Music oversaw the conversion of Pop art into Art Pop and back again – the total remix, the whole trip. With Ferry, Mackay and Eno all being from art school, as steeped in the components of Hamilton's list of pop cultural ingredients as they were in the soundscapes of the avant-garde (Mackay at Reading and Eno at Winchester, grooving to John Cage and La Monte Young), so Roxy Music would become a total Pop theatre, in which speed, time travel, labelling and romance would all play their parts in the final mix.

/ Brian Eno's definition of Pop, which he gave in an interview to *The Guardian* on the twenty-fifth anniversary of the release of Roxy Music's first album, could be seen to summarise – for the time being, at any rate – the founding philosophies of Pop's relation to art, and of Pop art's relation to both viewer and artist: 'I have never thought that pop was about making music in the traditional sense,' he said, 'it's about creating new, imaginary worlds and inviting people to join them.'

/ This is a statement which could almost provide the caption for Dexter Dalwood's paintings of popstar interiors, engaging as it does with that basic fairy-tale, sci-fi, androgyne other-worldliness that the best of Pop seems to define, from Pete Townshend's mascara to Prince's veil. In today's Warhol World of total Pop, where Pop is all the post-Pop kids have ever known, there is always the chance that someone five years ahead of us, with all the duty of youth, will be making yet another new imaginary world. It would be in the nature of these things.

NEIL TENNANT INTERVIEWED BY MICHAEL BRACEWELL

MB

/ What do you think the relationship between pop and art has been over the last, say, forty years? Your starter for ten. . .

/

NT

/ Well, the relationship goes back to the start of Pop art in the 1950s, when artists in Britain and America began to respond to pop music. If you take Britain, you think of Richard Hamilton and Peter Blake, who were obviously into Elvis and Little Richard. They appreciated the importance of these performers as icons, and they were presented as icons in their artwork. I mean, it's amazing how quickly art responded to pop, to the extent that only twelve years after the start of pop music with Elvis, Pop art was sort of burnt out, really. So I think it's a very close relationship. In Britain the relationship was particularly strengthened by the existence of foundation courses at art schools, so that your layabout pop star type, rather than having to get a job, could go and hang around an art college for a year or two, and take a mild interest in what was going on, which would influence what they did. So it's no accident that John Lennon went to art college – and did The Who go to art college? Because they were very self-consciously Pop art.

One of the Stones went to art college, didn't he? Then in the Seventies, of course, you've got Bryan Ferry studying with Richard Hamilton. Adam Ant went to art college. He was lectured by Allen Jones. I once introduced Allen Jones's first wife to Paul McCartney, and she said, 'Oh, I met you in the Sixties when I was married to Allen Jones,' and he said, 'Oh that's why I didn't recognise you, you were probably dressed as a coffee table then!' The Beatles had a real interest in contemporary art, particularly through their relationship to the art dealer Robert Fraser. Paul McCartney once told this story about Robert Fraser going round to his house, and McCartney had to disappear off somewhere, and when he came back, Fraser had left a little Magritte painting on the kitchen table, which I think said 'au revoir'.

/

MB

/ I always think it's a fairly good assumption that music that came from art colleges, or through art colleges, tends to be quite good.

/

NT

/ It does. But also pop musicians tend to like art, or they used to. I don't think they do so much now. And I like the way that people in pop music really enjoy the celebration of everyday life, artefacts and fame and all the rest of it. Because they're a part of it, they reflect that in their music, or they used to – it's the same sort of attitude found in Pop art. Also, pop musicians relish the easiness of it – the fact that it's just about an idea, because that's what pop music is. Pop music came along, and you didn't have to be trained at the Royal College of Music, or the Vienna Conservatory, you could have a basic knowledge and have ideas, and make a lot of noise. Sounds a bit easy and, in a way, it is a bit easy if you've got the ideas and the talent. And I think that's why pop

musicians are always attracted to Pop art. And it's mutual. Andy Warhol was fascinated by pop music, amazingly so, and then created a whole new kind of pop group, with The Velvet Underground. I always like it when pop music goes 'arty', and pop music always goes 'arty' rather than 'art'. Pop music likes the style of art as well; it likes the whole thing. Art is still emblematic of freedom, it really is. And people respond to that in music or, as I keep saying, they used to.

/

MB

/ What's been your professional experience of working with leading contemporary artists, such as Derek Jarman or Sam Taylor-Wood?

/

NT

/ Well, British people love pop music. People always find it terribly exciting, and artists are no different. It's one of the things I love about Britain, people take pop music terribly seriously, and that's what's interesting – contemporary art's become a bit like pop music, everyone's got an opinion on it. When you ask somebody to work with you, if they want to do it, they always find they get a totally different experience to what they'd get in the art world. So when we worked with Sam Taylor-Wood on our 'Somewhere' shows at the Savoy, that was really exciting for us. It was all Sam's idea. We had a completely different idea, actually. We wanted to have CCTV cameras all over London, projecting directly onto the stage. That's why it was called 'Somewhere' because we were just somewhere else. But it was too complicated to do. Anyway, Sam had the idea of the real time party. I don't know if she regards it as part of her work, but it was a really amazing event to stage. And I don't think it's like anything else Sam has done before, although it draws upon what she does, and of course it draws upon what we do, so it's a genuine collaboration. My point being that it's something that neither of us could have done without the other, so the parity is really important. What's really good is that it's presented as entertainment – no dealers and critics, which can be very liberating for the artist I think.

/

MB

/ It's interesting, when I was walking down here today, I was doing that thing where sometimes when you walk through London you feel like you're walking through your own autobiography, you know?

/

NT

/ Oh, endlessly.

/

MB

/ And I remember going to – it would probably have been the ICA, in about 1977 – so punk had kind of happened, but the seismic shock waves of punk were still very much being felt; and thinking that punk was maybe the last occasion in the UK when there seemed to be this fabulous coalition between the arts and music. And by the arts I mean critical writing, image making, the lot . . .

/

NT

/ There was a little bit of that, you know, in Brit Pop.

/

MB

/ That's interesting . . .

/

NT

/ Brit Pop was the last time we had artiness, you know, Blur were and are arty, Jarvis, very arty – well they all are in Pulp, actually. I think that the Pulp videos – I almost like them more than the records: *Disco 2000* and *Common People* – fantastic, unbelievable, pure Pop art. I think there have been phases where art and pop have really mixed. In the Sixties there was

definitely a two-way thing, a definite
response. And that happened in punk, too.
There was a scene there that people were
involved in, around Malcolm McLaren –
and Derek Jarman knew them because of
the whole Andrew Logan thing. I think a
very interesting phase in London, which
everyone overlooks, is the mid-Seventies
scene that led to punk. I think it's fascinating,
when you've got *Ritz* magazine, and you've
got Derek Jarman doing his thing out there
in the Docklands, and you've got the
Alternative Miss World happening, and
Bryan Ferry is around being glamorous.
Even Peter York's *Them* thing. You know, all
that was really fascinating, a sort of plastic
sandals period. Fiorucci and all that.
What's interesting is that it wasn't about
bands... it was Bowie and Roxy.
/
MB
/ And Lindsay Kemp doing *Flowers* at
the Roundhouse.
/
NT
/ Now the gap between glam-rock and
punk is fantastically short. Punk rock is
actually just a continuation of glam.
The sound, the clothes, it's a continuation
but it's a different kind of artifice. I mean
God Save the Queen is a great glam-rock

record, and so is *Pretty Vacant*, it's even
got a glam-rock lyric. In fact, it's sort of an
ironic glam-rock way of saying 'pretty'.
It's almost the Sweet doing *Ballroom Blitz* . . .
/
/ Also in punk rock, because of Malcolm
McLaren, you've got theory. You'd never
had theory in pop music. Actually, to be
quite honest, you kind of wonder whether it
was a good thing, but it was great for a short
period. But, you know, there was the whole
Situationist thing and with Roxy Music
you had art content and art references.
Bryan Ferry's second solo album cover is
a supreme piece of Pop art with the
swimming pool and everything. At the time
he had huge billboards of that image
around London, and it was wonderful to
see because it was so good, we all so
wanted to be by this Bel Air swimming pool.
That's another thing about pop music, by
the way, which everyone forgets – fly
posters. One of the great pleasures of pop
music is that you can ask the record
company to stick your poster all over
London, and they'll do it. Chris and I in
bowler hats with bowed heads – all over
London. You turn the street into an exhibition
space. It's great. And of course if you're
going to really spend the money, you could
have a huge billboard on Cromwell Road.
And there have been people who have
really appreciated the value of that over the
years. One of my favourite ones was by
David Bowie in Piccadilly Circus, thanking his
audience in 1973 with "Love on ya! David."
/
MB
/ Is it maybe true that the single most
significant bridge between pop music
and art over the last thirty years has been
David Bowie, in the collective imagination,
if not in fact?
/
NT
/ It depends whether you're going to
draw the distinction between art and arty.

Arty is having the style of art, and as we
were just saying, punk was the first thing
that brought theory into it. Not that it
necessarily has to have theory to be art.
You do something with the style of art, and
therefore you are arty. The sleeve of our first
album is an expression of minimalism in pop
music. A twelve inch square vinyl sleeve,
with a picture the size of a postage stamp in
the middle. But I wouldn't say it's art – I would
say it's arty. It thinks it has the style of art. It
wants to be looked at in a different way.
And that's why being arty is quite important,
because I've always thought pop music
divides into two things – and I've been
saying this since the mid-Eighties, by the
way: it's either aspirational Bowie/Roxy, or
it's regular guy-on-the-street, of which there
are too many examples to go into –
basically it's everyone else. But it's the
aspirational ones who use artiness to lift
themselves just above the industry norm,
trying to be special. Pop music really works
when it's made special through the arty
approach, it becomes almost magical.
/
MB
/ I was wondering whether you felt that
there are specific lessons that artists can
learn from pop?
/
NT
/ I actually think it would be better
nowadays if pop stars were more influenced
by art.
/
/
MB
/ Where do you feel the current
conservatism in much chart music is
coming from?
/
NT
/ It's a sort of market thing really.
I think people are sometimes presented with
the thought that pop music is something
that's happened, has a repertoire that you

sort of cover, it's Masterpiece Theatre as
pop music. And I think that's a real pity.
I think dithering around on the outskirts is
very interesting, but I like to engage in the
full-blooded commercial nightmare that is
the music industry, to try and use that
machinery. It's a great thing, you know,
you've got this vast machinery sending out
stuff all over the world, plastering your image
everywhere. But I just don't think people
see it as being about ideas any more.
If you listen to Adam Ant's singles from the
early 1980s and look at the imagery from
the first big album he had, it's really amazing
to think that these were records that were
number one in the charts. At the end of the
day they were very weird. *Ant Music* is a
very strange record. It sounds experimental
now. A few ideas go a long way in pop
music, you know.
/
MB
/ You once said that some people
seem to think that Pet Shop Boys records
kind of make themselves, with you and
Chris just sitting there reading a magazine
or something . . .
/
NT
/ That we make them look easy, yes.
/
MB
/ Do you think there are any analogies
between . . .
/
NT
/ Between that and art? Oh, totally.
I think that some people think about certain
works of art, 'Oh this is too easy.' I mean it
isn't necessarily easy, and it takes years of
experience to distil what you know into
what you create. Creating simplicity in art
is the most difficult thing to do. Writing an
exhilarating three-and-a-half minute pop
song over an ancient chord change and
somehow making it sound fresh and new
is pure inspiration.

post-punk group, and at one time you could look at the charts and think, 'they're good, they're shit, they're good, they're shit' – and what you really meant was, 'they're sort of punk', by which you meant they had absolute integrity in what they did and were not just a commercial sell-out. And at some point, quite recently, that connection was lost. But unusually nothing has replaced it. Maybe that's a good thing, just to like music on it's own terms. But I think a whole sense of commitment and meaning is lost when music is like that, when the ideology has gone from it. Because all you are then presented with is a series of choices that aren't based on ideology or theory, or a deeply held core of beliefs – they are just choices. So you could do anything, you know.

/

MB

/ There's a video piece in this exhibition by Mark Leckey called *Fiorucci Made Me Hardcore* which is essentially a montage of film clips of crowds at dance events, and it seems to have all the melancholy of a certain kind of biography or nostalgia. In fact, it makes you think that a lot of dance music is deeply melancholy.

/

NT

/ I can take anything and make it sound melancholy.

/

MB

/ You don't think dance music, per se is on the sad side?

/

NT

/ Well we're back to the famous happy-sad music – we used to call this style of music happy-sad music – and, on the dance floor, you can feel quite exhilarated while feeling very, very sad, in a weird kind of way. But the issue here is actually drugs. Because dance music is a drug-based form, a lot of it is made to be heard through the

filter of drugs – not all of it, but a lot of it. I mean, your Wigan Northern Soul people were all on speed, anyway, that didn't really affect your hearing, it just gave you stamina to carry on. Ecstasy has of course created a particular kind of music.

/

MB

/ I remember once asking Bridget Riley about this, because of the way her early Op Art pictures were seen as somehow trippy.

/

NT

/ You didn't need to smoke anything in front of a Bridget Riley. When they had her show at the Serpentine Gallery, I spent about quarter of an hour walking towards and away from one of those pictures, because I liked the weird effect, it made me feel physically strange.

/

MB

/ Did you get to the bit where you see a violet line going through the bottom third of the painting?

/

NT

/ Yeah, it's great! I mean, that's what we all like about Bridget Riley. I seem to think she didn't aim to do that though.

/

MB

/ It's strange how art and pop become linked to personal memory. I thought your song *Being Boring* was like an audit on a generation.

/

NT

/ Well, it's about aspirations for your life, isn't it? So, yes, I think it probably is. Although for a lot of people it's Andy Warhol who is still an audit for our lives, really. So much has followed on from Andy Warhol, it's incredible.

/

MB

/ I'm fully paid up on that thing that we are

/

MB

/ Do you think that there are works of contemporary art that have the qualities of a perfectly constructed pop song?

/

NT

/ Well, recently, in Sam Taylor-Wood's exhibition at White Cube, I thought that about her speeded up film of a bowl of fruit rotting. You think, 'Why has no-one done that before?' and with the perfect pop song you normally think, 'Why has no-one written that before?' It seems so obvious. And Sam's idea obviously draws on still life, but it's really a gorgeous and beautiful idea, it encapsulates what seventy percent of art is about, i.e. life and death, in one amazing film, which is also presented as a painting.

/

MB

/ Do you think it's now getting harder for works of art or pop music to escape being 'just another look' with the whole post-modern bombardment of media and advertising, and so on?

/

NT

/ The problem nowadays is the lack of ideology, and I think this is very true of pop music. The Pet Shop Boys are a

living in Warhol's world, actually. He did
get it right, I think.
/
NT
/ Yes, I think he got it right, whether by
intellect or instinct, or just by being part of
it, he definitely got it right. Although he was
more innocent about things than people
are now. Andy Warhol wasn't ironic in the
way it's used nowadays – about fame,
for instance. He had a genuine gee-whiz
quality, didn't he? And I used to love
Interview magazine, when it was: "Andy and
Bob Colacello go and interview Diana Ross",
and say, 'Oh, you're fabulous!' And she says,
'Thank you.' 'I loved that fur coat you wore
in the second half.' 'Oh, yes, it's great.
Bob Mackie designed it.' I was thrilled that
Bob Mackie designed Liza's wedding dress.
I was absolutely thrilled.
/
MB
/ Did you go by the way?
/
NT
/ No, we didn't go because we were
doing CD UK, and you've got to get your
priorities right.
/
End of Interview, 28 March 2002

ENTERING ARTISTS
36–37

BOTTLE RACK
36

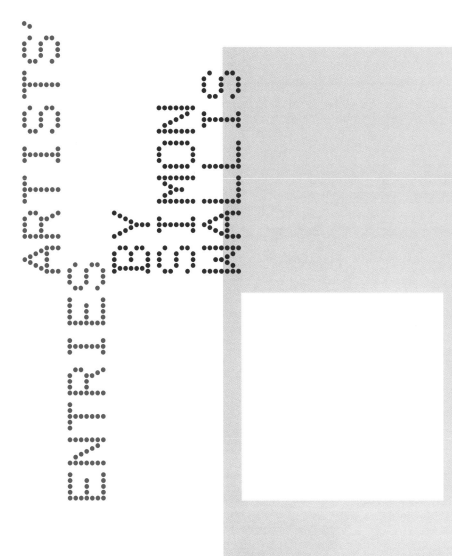

remix (re)mix

DOUG AITKEN
FIONA BANNER
VANESSA BEECROFT
CANDICE BREITZ
ANGELA BULLOCH
DAN GRAHAM
ANDREAS GURSKY
GARY HUME
MIKE KELLEY
WOLF
ELIZABETH PEYTON
SAM SMALLWOMANS
WOLFGANG TILLMANS
GAVIN TURK
GILLIAN WEARING

DOUG AITKEN

01 Hysteria
1998

Doug Aitken's *Hysteria* provides a short
visual history of the mass adulation of
rock 'n' roll bands and the crowd mentality
it encourages. The remixed archive film
footage focuses on the wild abandon
of audiences working themselves into
a frenzy of desire through four decades
of pop. It includes Beatles-era screamers
losing control and clutching their heads
in their hands, Hippies and Hell's Angels
mixing at an outdoor concert,
choreographed arm waving and clapping,
crowd surfing and the homoerotic violence
of mosh pits. In the early 1960s, audiences
liberated from the rigours of post-war life

developed a hedonistic appreciation
of pop and its performers that was to sow
the seeds for more radical and political
stances later in the decade. Becoming a
pop music fan became an important rite
of passage, one that bound young people
together and showed them the power
of different aesthetic choices and
experiences. The importance of pop
within youth culture was fuelled by new
marketing techniques that heightened
desire and enabled the rise of the teenager
as an economic, cultural and political
force. Newly mediated products including
music, films, fashion and magazines could
now be geared towards this market.
The youthful crowd mentality that
developed from pop consumption enacts
an almost religious ritual as music generates
a state of primal ecstasy and loss of self-
control. This is intensified in close proximity
to pop celebrities, who are created as a
protean distillation of our needs and desires.
These performers, however, remain
unseen in Aitken's piece as, this time, it is
the audience who is the star of the show.

FIONA BANNER

Don't Look Back
1999

Fiona Banner's *Don't Look Back* comprises three texts that describe from memory DA Pennebaker's seminal 1967 'rockumentary' *Don't Look Back*, whose subject was Bob Dylan's legendary first British tour in 1965. This film was instrumental in helping to create the fan and media mythology that surrounds Dylan as an artist and performer. It also features a seminal moment in pop iconography, in which Dylan holds up cards with words that relate to his song *Subterranean Homesick Blues*, each card being discarded after every line is sung. Banner turns her mental pictures of Dylan into a stream of words written in the present tense, as if she were there with him at his concerts. Her descriptions, each remembering the film slightly differently, are printed in a black sans serif typeface onto silver paper applied directly to the wall, as though they were fly-posted concert posters. From a distance the words take on the appearance of people in a large crowd, putting the viewer in the position of a performer looking out onto them. The text is arranged so as to encourage movement between the physicality of the words on the paper and their curiously ambivalent legibility. The texts often highlight the different remixed rhythms and cadences of American English compared to the stiff formality of its British counterpart. Banner's work highlights the slippages and preferences of memory in creating pop celebrity. She formally builds this into the work through variances in description and the difficulty of reading her texts in a coherent manner, due to the length of the sentences and their dense arrangement. *Don't Look Back* emphasises the process of media myth-making that surrounds pop artists, where every utterance and quip is given undue significance and personas are seen as being authentic and unique. Banner explores her fan worship of Dylan and the disappointments to which it may lead as musical heroes get older and the pop fictions that surround them are encroached upon by reality.

HROUGH LONDON, ... THEY'RE GOING ... THEY ARE RIGHT ... EVEN WAN
UN, SENDING UP BOB. THEY'RE AWFUL AND THEY ARE RIGHT ... EVEN WAN
RE PILLARS. THE BAND'S AWFUL AND HE SAYS HE DOESN'T WANT IT, DOESN'T EVEN WAN
OLK BAND AND HE SAYS HE DOESN'T WANT IT, WEARING RAYBANS AND CLICK
HERE, SHE'S BEAUTIFUL, BUT YOU CAN ONLY SEE HALF OF HER. L
T THE BACK BOTH SMOKING AND WEARING RAYBANS AND CLICK
HE TYPEWRITER PLAYING IT LIKE ITS A KEYBOARD, SHAKING HI
ORD', BOB ASKS ALBERT IF HE KNOWS THAT SONG I DIED FROM
ASN'T GOT AN ENDING FOR THE SONG HE'S WRITING YET AND
RANSFIXED BY HER, OR HER VOICE. HE'S JUST STARING ACROSS
BOUT DONOVAN, THERE MUST BE SOMETHING ABOUT HIM IN THE
YLAN ASKS WHAT HE'S LIKE. THE GUY FROM THE ANIMALS IS DOWI
EING SICK AND HE LAUGHS. THE GUY FROM THE ANIMALS IS DOWI
ROM A BOTTLE, HE SAYS THAT DONOVAN'S ALL RIGHT, IN HIS NEW
E DESERTED HIS FANS DIDN'T HE? THAT'S THE HEADLINE.'DONOV
NOTHER CAR, THEY PASS A SIGN FOR THE GIG, IT SAYS SOLD OU
ECAUSE HE MUST STICK OUT HIS HEAD OUT OF THE WINDOW. IT'S
EAR TO LOOK AT HIM. HE DOES AUTOGRAPHS. HE GOES ON IN LIV
EALLY PUSHED BACK, MILES AWAY, AND THEN SOMEONE GOES PS
UT WHISPERING AND THEN THEY PLUG IN ANOTHER LEAD AND
LAPPING. THE SECOND NUMBER IS, 'IN THE DIME STORES AND B
O SUCCESS LIKE FAILURE AND FAILURE IS NO SUCCESS AT ALL',
HERE. HIS GUITAR IS SLUNG LOW. HE LOOKS SO SMALL, HE'S NO
ONDON, STANDING IN FRONT OF THE GUITAR SHOP LOOKING AT
OOK LIKE BOXES WITH STICKS ON THE END. DYLAN SAYS HE WISH
N ONE OF THE WINDOWS IN SIGN PAINT ABOUT DYLAN, IT LOOKS
HEY HAVEN'T GOT ONES LIKE THIS IN NEW YORK. STILL IN DENM
IGARS. THE GUY WITH THE LONG FACE IS ON THE PHONE: HE SA'
R. DYLAN, AND I THINK HE MIGHT UNTIE HIMSELF, WELL WHAT IS
ANAGER MR ALBERT GROSSMAN HERE AND HE'D VERY MUCH LIK
UGE DESK INFRONT. THERE'S SOME MORE CHAT ON THE PHONE,
AY WELL WE WANT TO DO THE SHOW WITH YOU, BUT WE'RE IN A
HAT YOU CAN COME UP WITH, THANKYOU, ETC. THEN HE GETS
AN I HAVE A TRY, HE GETS ON, HI WELL WE SPOKE IN NEW YORK
O FIND OUT THAT YOUR ONLY OFFERING HALF, OK SPEAK LATER
ENSE BUT PLEASED AIR OF CONSPIRACY ABOUT IT, IT GOES LIKE
HE SAME MONEY, THEY SEEM PLEASED, IN ANGE
ET UP LIKE AN INTERVIEW

01

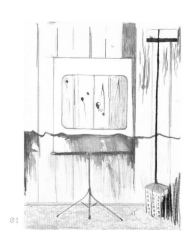

01

JULIE BECKER 43

01 Untitled
1999
02 Untitled
2002

Julie Becker's *Suburban Legend* examines the rumoured links between the family favourite film *The Wizard of Oz* and Pink Floyd's album *Dark Side of the Moon*, both of which contain the opposing qualities of self-discovery and child-like escapism. Since the early 1970s, American teenagers have spent time trying to synch the record with the movie, following a suburban myth that Pink Floyd wrote *Dark Side of the Moon* as an alternative soundtrack. The synching is supposed to begin with the third roar of the MGM lion at the beginning of the film. Prompted by a user's manual written by Becker, viewers of *Suburban Legend* are invited to scroll through the video to link up the best bits. Becker engages with the domestic consumption of pop that allows ritual recombinations of trippy favourites to accompany and enhance hanging-out or getting high or drunk. This atmosphere increases the mystique and experience of music and generates nostalgia for a counter-culture that may once have been more radical and subversive than its ersatz suburban incarnation. Both of the works with which Becker plays are seen as classics of their genre. They have a highly psychedelic quality which holds an enduring fascination for viewers and listeners who turn to them to temporarily find themselves, like Dorothy, radically elsewhere.

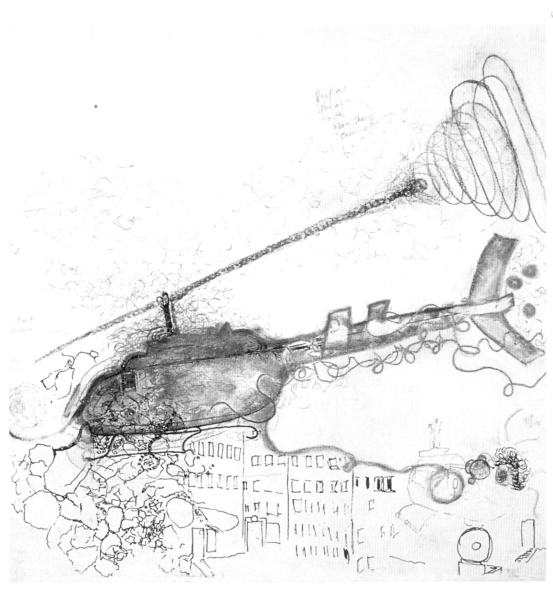

ANDREA BOWERS

01 Democracy's Body -
Dance Dance Revolution
2001

Andrea Bowers' *Dance Dance
Revolution* explores the cult following in
suburban Los Angeles of a karaoke dance
routine machine, where players dance
together or perform solo to a mixture of
American pop or Japanese 'dancemania'.
The performances are captivatingly
complex and reveal a highly competitive
aspect of dance. The game demonstrates
the rapid development of interactivity, as it
requires the players to use their whole body
rather than merely the twitching wrist and
thumb action demanded by older video
games. Bowers captures the adrenalin-
fuelled intensity and pleasure that playing
this game gives to both performers and
spectators. One scene focuses on a
young girl dressed in a Superman T-shirt
and baggy hip hop pants that drape over
her grubby shelltops. We watch her
experience with the game unfolding as she
gives herself over to the competitive dance.
Her feet stomp in complex patterns on the
lit up dancefloor platform that directs the
moves and it's a captivating sight to see
someone so engrossed and unselfconscious
in their enjoyment. The footage starts in real
time and then slows down, as does the
phased soundtrack, which includes samples
from the game itself and music used by the
Judson Dance Theatre in the mid 1960s,
comprising compositions by John Cage
and La Monte Young.

Another player has a much more
fixated and serious stance as he runs
through a routine of aggressive stabbing
jolts, his shoulders snapping back and forth.
The rest of the footage flits through different
combinations of partners competing
together on the machine, many of whom
look sweaty and exhausted. The soundtrack
mirrors the disorientating arcade
environment of flashing lights and meshing
noises as these players run through hybrid
dance routines using tap, jazz,
breakdancing, ballet and aerobics. Bower's
work highlights the excitement of dance
music, bodily interaction with technology
and the collective mentality that develops
around these pop-driven crazes.

CANDICE BREITZ 05

01 Double Karen (Close to You)
2000

Candice Breitz uses sampling techniques to cut and paste material drawn from pop music videos or performances. *Double Karen* uses manipulated footage of Karen Carpenter, shown on two video monitors, to make it appear as if she is singing a severely edited duet with herself. It features the classic song *(They Long To Be) Close to You* written by Burt Bacharach and Hal David in 1970, edited to concentrate exclusively on the words 'me' and 'you'. Breitz strips the song down to the relationship between the listener and the performer, which has a built-in fantasy of togetherness and intimacy. Carpenter's beautiful crystal-clear voice is chopped up to describe a stuttering, dysfunctional relationship that seems to reflect what some of us know of her tragic death from a heart attack resulting from a long running battle with anorexia. Carpenter's androgynous look and limp-wristed drumming are visually jarring against the song, whose lyrics and melody we can easily flesh out, so enduringly familiar are Carpenters records from three decades on the airwaves. The fascination of the piece is added to by seeing such a thoroughly asexual woman singing one of the most tender love songs in pop while playing the drums, a largely male dominated instrument. This imagery, and the highly crafted nature of their records, has made The Carpenters, in equal measure, a sincere and ironic touchstone for a vast array of pop acts. Breitz unsentimentally probes into the emotional construction of pop and allows us to ponder the formula of a love song, the mental state of the artist singing it, and our relationship to them as music consumers.

ANGELA BULLOCH

Disco Floor_Bootleg:16
2002

sequences relating to the different
parts of the soundtrack. These comprise
complex mixed colours changing at
regular one second intervals, along with
an overlay of primary colours that fade and
rise according to the second simultaneous
interfering sound layer. The soundtrack uses
a remix of Chic's seminal disco track *Good
Times* whose infectious Bernard Edwards'
bassline was sampled by The Sugarhill
Gang and Grandmaster Flash in the early
development of hip hop. Other bass tones
are also overlaid to create parallel systems
and references and a remixed confusion of
sound and vision. The digital time code
of the modules works against and alongside
the subtle timing differences in the music.
Although *Disco Floor_Bootleg:16* references
dance music, people are not allowed
onto the work, they have to engage with the
complex choreography of coloured light
at a distance.

Since 1999 Bulloch has arranged her
pixel box modules into various combinations
including towers, rows and screens.
Her work has a remixing mentality that
engages with systems of organisation
using varied methods that don't necessarily
develop chronologically. She runs
simultaneous practices that have included:
drawing machines that react to movement,
pressure or sounds; sound and light works;
photographs and texts. Her works use the
contingent structures of life as material to
be reconfigured and reinterpreted.

Angela Bulloch's Pixel Box DMX modules
are a collaboration with Holger Friese.
Together they created a modular light
mixing system that allows 1.6 million colours
to be mixed from fluorescent tubes in three
screen colours, red, green and blue.
An interface was designed to operate
the module individually with digital
information and each work runs its own
programme. *Disco Floor_Bootleg:16*
consists of sixteen waxed beech wood DMX
modules in a four by four arrangement, with
pixels facing upwards so that they assume
the appearance of a lighted disco floor.
The piece runs with two animated

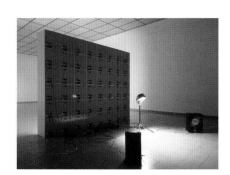

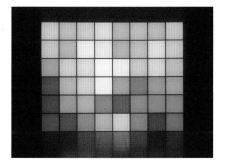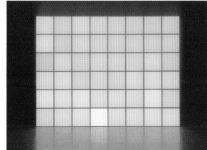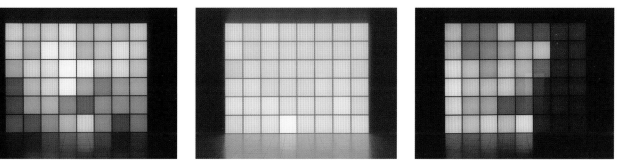

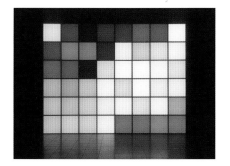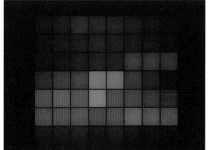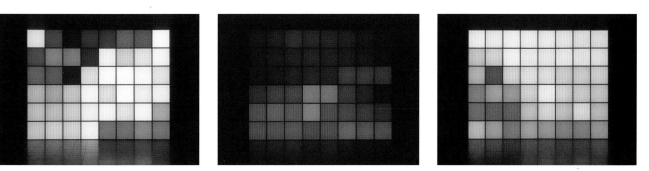

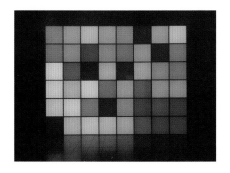

DEXTER DALWOOD

01 Paisley Park
1998
02 Neverland
(Michael Jackson's Bedroom)
1999
03 Ian Curtis' Bedroom
2001

Dexter Dalwood's paintings of the interiors of pop stars' homes, including *Paisley Park*, *Ian Curtis' Bedroom* and *Neverland*, play on a 'through the keyhole' fascination for the life of celebrities, while remixing eclectic references to the history of painting. We are curious about those we idolise as their lives seem exciting, mysterious and desirable, an attitude fuelled by endless media speculation. Dalwood's paintings evoke both our memories of music and the pop myths of our time. His work contains an intrinsic interest in the private spaces of the famous, using a witty and knowing reinterpretation of

seventeenth and eighteenth century history painting – a genre that functions similarly to contemporary media by hyping and aggrandising legendary incidents and characters. This reworking of art historical material was developed in the late 1950s and early 60s by artists with a close relation to pop culture such as Richard Hamilton, David Hockney and Michael Andrews. Dalwood's work updates this attitude by referencing cultural agendas that are without a clear-cut hierarchy in a media situation that gives as much coverage and attention to pop celebrities as world leaders.

Dalwood's paintings engage with pop personalities by depicting their empty private rooms that would normally be shielded from prying eyes. The prurience of the viewer has been encouraged by celebrity magazine features on the homes of the rich and famous, and Dalwood paints his pictures from collages he creates that riff on these glossy fantasies. What does Michael Jackson get up to in his bedroom? Does Prince like to contemplate his platinum and gold discs while flower-arranging? Formally, Dalwood has a magpie mentality directed towards art and pop. He recombines his trans-historical references into new painterly fictions that allow the viewer to vacillate between an appreciation of how the painting is made and its narrative implications.

RINEKE DIJKSTRA

01 The Buzz Club, Liverpool (UK)
and Mysteryworld, Zaandam (NL)
1996

Rineke Dijkstra's *The Buzz Club/Mysteryworld* is a set of intimate, awkward, touching and funny video portraits of teenagers dancing in a white clinical booth that the artist set up for one night in a club in Liverpool and in Zaandam in the Netherlands. It perfectly reflects the mentality of teenagers who are lost in their own world, temporarily removed from the authority of adults. Dijkstra's subjects are people on the verge of adulthood, experimenting with personas and their emerging sexuality. They use all the trappings of adult leisure as props, particularly drinking and smoking, but still don't carry any convincing sense of ease in the world, as nothing for them is yet fully formed.

/ Each person in Dijkstra's film represents, by default, a different aspect of ephemeral fashion and attitude, which has already rapidly dated since she made the work in the mid 1990s. The girls pluck up courage to dance and show off their bodies and sexuality, the boys try to appear cool, macho and hard. A sense of attitude, identity and performance is crucial to the enjoyment of clubs – it allows one to escape more fully from the pressures of daily living and the new responsibilities that adulthood brings. Dijkstra has created a captivating portrait of youth that bears close attention; being in turns charming, hilarious and revealing.

RODNEY GRAHAM

Phonokinetoscope
2001

Rodney Graham's *Phonokinetoscope* comprises a turntable, vinyl record, amp, speakers and a 16mm projector. The turntable and projector are linked so that when the needle is on the record the projector starts. Accompanied by a psychedelic rock soundtrack performed by Graham, the film shows him taking a tab of LSD and riding his bicycle through the Tiergarten in Berlin. It invites the viewer to share from the outside an altered mental landscape that is a cryptic, multi-layered re-enactment of the first acid trip taken by the inventor of LSD, Dr Albert Hofmann in 1943. It is also inspired by Thomas Edison's

invention of the Kinetophonograph in 1889, which was an early form of cinema capable of showing a moving picture in synchronisation with recorded music.

/ Graham's journey begins with the pouring of a cup of tea from a thermos flask inscribed with the words 'Sunflower Shanghai'. The film shows his drug-altered attention being caught by the minutiae of everyday objects such as a playing card, a spring-loaded wooden clothes peg and a bicycle rack. After noticing a Queen of Diamonds playing card on the ground he attaches it to the spokes of his bicycle wheel so that it flicks repeatedly as he rides. He stops his leisurely trip around the park to gaze up at a statue before finally riding his bike backwards over a bridge. The tune Graham performs as a soundtrack to his film is a mournful ditty of mild melancholy with acoustic guitar strumming and periods of wild squally electric guitar that recall Pink Floyd's soundtrack contributions to Michaelangelo Antonioni's 1970 film *Zabriskie Point*. The work seems to have many references that may or may not be meaningful and can be equally ignored or pondered as we go along with the song and his cycle ride. Psychedelic drugs have played an important part in the development of pop and film from the 1960s onwards and the supposed 'expanded consciousness' found its most convincing and enduring manifestations in these artforms. Graham plays with the clichéd language of drugs and pop, presenting the viewer with a prosaic vision of mild-mannered eccentricity and dopey self-indulgence that, although eschewing the usual visual pyrotechnics associated with hallucinogenic drugs and rock 'n' roll, is nevertheless curiously captivating.

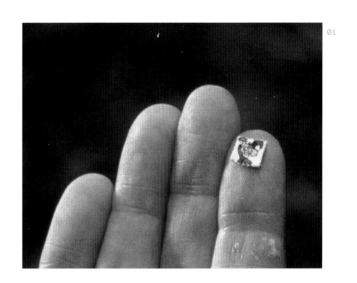

ANDREAS GURSKY

01 May Day IV
2000

The dancing masses of people illustrate a shift between individualism and a collective tribalism. They display endless variations of utility clothing, exposed flesh, gesticulation and expression as they subdivide into self-absorbed dancers, romantic couples and adrenalin-fuelled clusters. Gursky seems to glean from this an underlying pattern in which the attention of the crowd is attracted towards whatever is being presented on stage, although that focal point remains outside of the picture.

Gursky's image operates on a level of abstraction, reminiscent of a large Jackson Pollock painting from the 1950s, as the viewer takes in the totality of the crowd and the small areas of colour that punctuate it. But Gursky also retains the narrative detail that allows us to single out individuals and identify what they are doing. He offers something expansive with this work, an empathy with situations that become greater than the sum of their parts. *May Day IV* presents a way of standing outside an experientially intense event and letting vision become both intoxicating and clinical in taking in the whole image and identifying its individual parts.

Andreas Gursky's large-scale photograph *May Day IV* captures a crowd of people packed together, milling around or dancing in a way that seems to ebb and flow with lines of energy, despite being a static image. The viewer can pick out faces and characters in this scene of a 'leisure army' cutting loose and having a good time. Gursky's human panorama offers up frozen vignettes that imply a soundtrack we can add imaginatively from our own experiences. He is fascinated by the spectacular quality of large crowds and takes up a god's eye view looking down on people as they throng together.

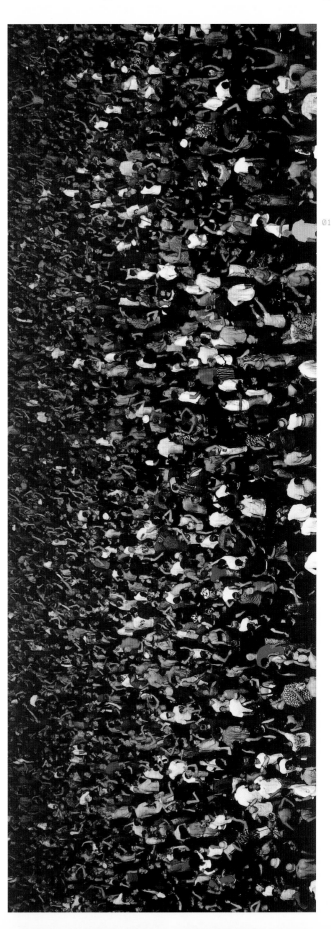

GARY HUME

01 Michael
2001

Gary Hume's paintings of Patsy Kensit, the definitive, serial 'rock-chick' girlfriend, and Michael Jackson are beautiful and intriguing images that lodge easily in the memory. Patsy Kensit is a particularly British media phenomenon who has gained fame as an actress, singer in 80s pop band Eighth Wonder, and pop star girlfriend. Jackson has lived out his entire life through pop, generating endless image changes which have resulted ultimately in a radical remixing of his own physicality. Hume's paintings are unusual as portraits because they seem to distil the highly mediated personalities of their subjects, but are neither aggrandising nor glibly ironic in so doing. There is, by necessity given the subjects, a curiously vacuous quality to these paintings that comes from our over-familiarity with Jackson's mask-like face – which, nevertheless, continues to arrest attention wherever his image appears - and Kensit's delicate English beauty, often used to add an easy glamour to gossip pages and TV shows. Hume's works contain a wry and sensitive insight into celebrity images and media personas without being didactic or illustrative. These paintings function in unexpected and subtle ways: bubblegum pink Patsy girlishly sucks or bites her thumb through green lips, and Michael has a drawn, skull-like white face framed with limp strands of hair, a macabre pinched nose, plaintive eyes and bright red sexually incongruous lips. The gloss paint of these works hints at Jackson's and Kensit's self-conscious and conflicted sense of beauty, as well as their tawdry veneer of showmanship – all of which comprise a seductive part of pop life and art.

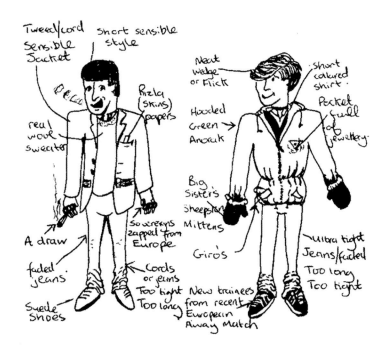

01

01

02

DAWN
MELLOR

Dawn Mellor's paintings of Madonna, Britney Spears and Courtney Love examine the camp, and near caricature, quality of these female stars through their highly sexualised pop personas. Madonna and Courtney have both played with various tropes of female sexuality including whore, dominatrix, nun, little girl and rock chick, remixing personas to appeal to a fickle and hungry media industry and easily bored audiences. Britney plays similar sartorial games underpinned by the public knowledge of her declared virginity, which adds to a heightened sense of desire for her and the often sexually teasing music she produces. There is an implied desire and fandom for these sexual objects in Mellor's decision to paint them. Courtney Love is depicted prone on the ground accepting the amorous advances of a large bear, as if she is up for anything and capable of being powerfully playful. She is draped with jewellery and wears ripped fishnet stockings with suspenders and high heels in a parody of prostitution and sexual availability. Madonna stands in a crucifixion pose wearing a red diamante cowboy outfit, blood dripping from her fingers while a set of wild dogs tears meat apart at her feet. Britney Spears holds the leads of a row of lapdogs with a startled look in her eyes and an unconvincing All American smile, as if facing over-zealous fans and pushy paparazzi. Mellor's paintings catalogue the bricolage of cultural references that these pop stars recycle for their changing images, which are used to help prolong interest in otherwise notoriously short careers. Mellor recycles and sidesteps the slickness of corporate pop and gives it a faux naif twist that embodies our ambivalence towards pop iconography and its language of easily distilled desire.

01

CHRIS OFILI 14

01 Popcorn Shells
1996
02 Afrodizzia
1996

Chris Ofili's energetic paintings heavily reference pop music history and sampling. *Afrodizzia* features hundreds of black faces ordered and interwoven in a cosmic storm of colour and carefully applied decoration. Some of the faces emerge allowing them to be fully recognised such as James Brown, Louis Armstrong, Michael Jackson or Little Richard. Names are spelt out onto clumps of elephant dung that have been attached to the canvas as if 'call-outs' of respect to major cultural figures, many of whom have left their indelible mark on pop history. Ofili's painting captures much of the energy and excitement of the music that he name-checks. The collaging and intermingling of a universe of black stars is both homage and a form of inspiration in itself, giving his paintings an improvisational lyricism. Ofili's work makes it clear that we must respect and acknowledge our traditions if we are to use them as a resource, something that hip hop culture has long done in its playful exploitation of samples and eclectic recombinations that demand musical expertise. *Afrodizzia* embodies many different tempos punctuated with a panoply of decoration, as if listening to a blistering solo played by Charlie Parker, Art Tatum, Sonny Rollins or Jimi Hendrix. Ofili's paintings contain the inspirational power of music and show how the cut and paste mentality can be used to great aesthetic effect. These works have an almost psychedelic hit to them, where the brain has to deal with too much information and every element suddenly appears hyperreal in an effort of recognition. This is the mind-altering effect of music captured in painting as it takes us elsewhere and excites the body and imagination.

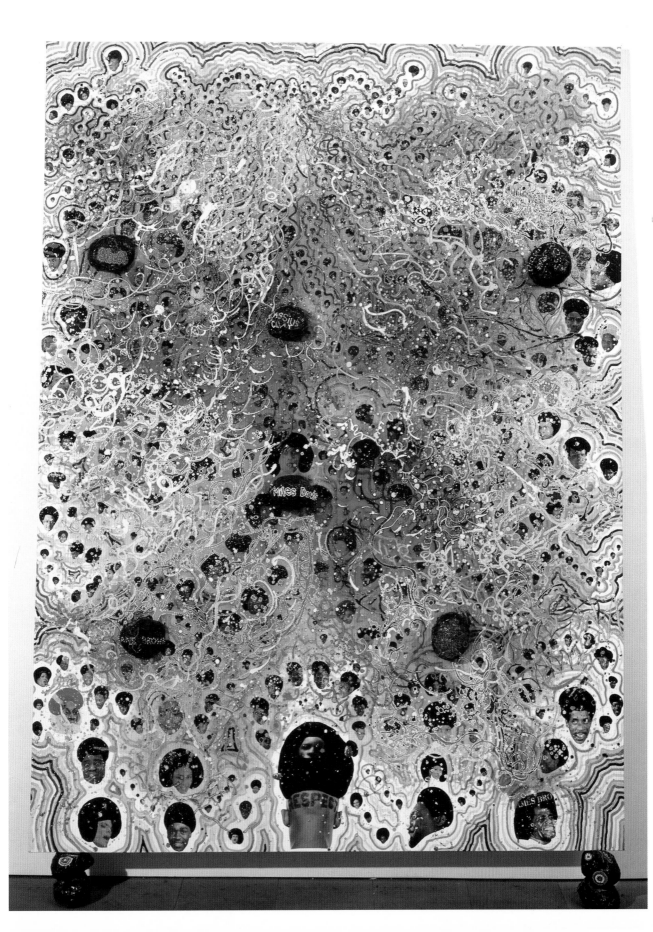

01

JULIAN OPIE 15

01 Damon from Blur
2000
02 engines-footsteps-voices
1999

Julian Opie's work embodies the principle of remixing and he has said 'I would rather combine and manipulate existing languages than try to invent a new one.' His graphically reductive and simplified image of an airport runway and cloudy sky, *engines-footsteps-voices*, has a romantic escapist quality that is added to through a soundtrack by St. Etienne, an influential pop group for whom Opie has produced several CD covers in the last few years. There is an easy listening jet-setting vibe to this work, evoking a sense of relaxation and escape that slows the viewer down. Easy listening has many connections to the chill-out and ambient sounds often used as an antidote to the hedonistic extremes of clubbing, while also serving as an aural backdrop to domestic leisure time when we switch off and simply drift. Opie's images have an instantly appealing clarity that transforms everyday scenes by smoothing out the rough edges of life and making all manner of people, places and things easily consumable and highly desirable.

/ Opie's portraits are developed from photographs he takes, reworked via the computer to use minimal detail in conveying the uniqueness of each subject's face. Opie's portraits of Blur provided a highly successful and memorable cover to their *Best of* album, continuing the tradition of artists producing pop album covers such as those designed for The Beatles' *Sergeant Pepper's Lonely Hearts Club Band* and *The White Album* by, respectively, Peter Blake and Richard Hamilton, or Warhol's *Sticky Fingers* for The Rolling Stones. Opie highlights the importance of a clearly recognisable image to aid the consumption and identity of music and his work harnesses the democratic and highly adaptable power of public signage in a playful blurring of visual languages.

01

02

ELIZABETH PEYTON

Elizabeth Peyton creates somewhat idealised portraits of celebrities and friends and has said that she never paints anyone she does not admire. The paintings have an intimacy in both scale and execution with a fan's attention to detail that is an obvious reflection of Peyton's sincere feelings towards her subjects, who have included Liam Gallagher, Sid Vicious and Kurt Cobain. She paints from photographs, which might serve to distance her yet further from those she depicts, but somehow it seems to have the opposite effect on the work. Peyton's paintings, although hardly didactic, emphasise how we begin to build our own personal relationship to celebrities through consuming and contemplating their images. We fantasise about what type of people they are as a natural extension of appreciating their music, and we want to know more about them to get closer to creativity, fame and the desirous excitement of pop. Painting appears to restore a wider spectrum of human emotions to the mediated images we are used to seeing. The adept feel Peyton has for her medium, coupled with the scale at which she works, allows us to reframe these individuals and what we might know of them. She makes her subjects appear tenderer than we perhaps expect. For instance, the brash bravado of male sexuality in the pop personas of Kurt Cobain and Liam Gallagher is smoothed out, allowing a feminised quality to emerge. The fact that these images are so painterly makes their subjects appear memorialised – sometimes before their time – by freezing the temporal rush and contingency of pop, while highlighting the effects that different media have on our perceptions of personality and pop iconography.

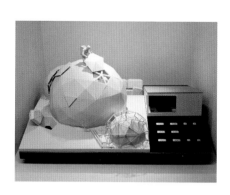

01

RICKY SWALLOW 17

Upgrade and Afterlife /
Four Demonstration Models
2001
01 Another Endless Excavation
2001
02 Model for Meticulous Maintenance
2001
03 Modeling the Marantz Experiment
2001
04 Wronging the Robots
2001

Ricky Swallow's turntable models are an ongoing project, started in 1997, concerned with creating miniature portable scenes recalling his favourite moments from science fiction films and local museum displays. The use of turntables brings the models into real time, enabling their multi-layered hobbyist narratives to unfold. The turning motion is like a video loop, extending time while halting the final outcome of the action. It's as though the needle is stuck in the groove in an endless present defined by the rotation and twitching of forms. This attitude recalls the earlier 'turntablist' mentality of DJs Kool Herc and Grandmaster Flash who warped time and sound to create new sonic fictions on their decks. The essentially redundant technology of the turntable in the digital age is given new life by Swallow as he remixes chronologies and references.

/ Swallow's models are at a scale of 1:24, bleached down to various shades of grey to allow an appreciation of their detailed handmade components and the film-still scenes they depict. The scale of the models closely resembles the reproductions that have influenced his work, which are taken from journals and science fiction publications. Here again is a parallel with the fantasies created by musicians and DJs involved in fusion, hip hop, techno and electro pop – particularly Herbie Hancock, Dr Octogan, Afrika Bambaataa, Derrick May and Carl Craig who evoked the technological future as a form of radical departure and creative possibility. The design of Swallow's models often suggests the nature of the narrative, which is in turn influenced by the architecture of the turntable he uses. For instance, moulded features, vents, buttons and tone arms are built into the structure of the scenes that Swallow depicts. They predict a future world where balances sway between human and robotic revolutions, as they do in the development of electronic music. In Swallow's models, individuals struggle in isolation to keep their worlds turning as they play with new ideas about evolution, remixing past, present and future.

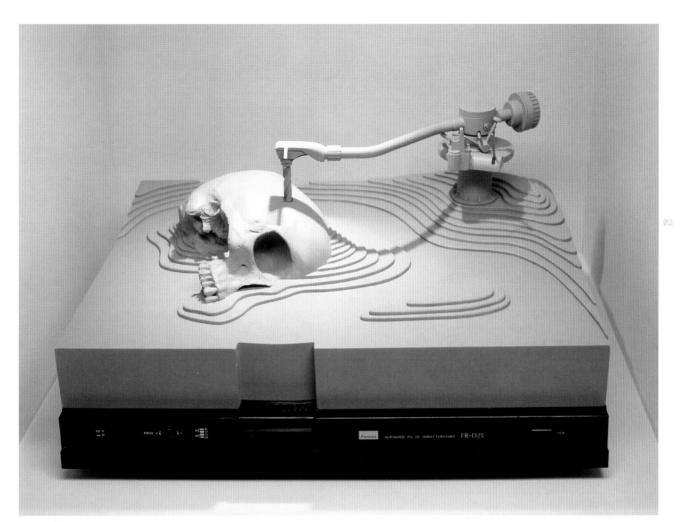

02

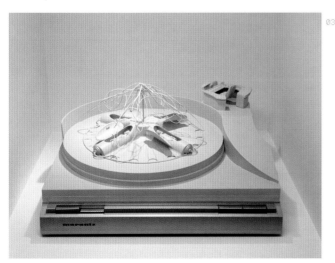

03

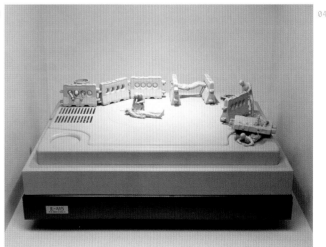

04

01

02

WOLFGANG TILLMANS

01 Miss Kittin
2001
02 303 in grass
1993
03 Mental Picture #52
2000

Wolfgang Tillmans' photographs are suffused with the spirit and inspiration of music, which creates a multiplicity of shifting associations and contexts. Colour, light and composition have close and deliberate correlations with melody and rhythm in his highly contingent work. Tillmans readily acknowledges the power of music, as it offers a paradigm for aesthetic freedom to play and recombine whilst celebrating the diversity and intensity of bodily experience in the world. His photographs vacillate between seductive abstractions, revealing portraits and heightened perceptions of everyday situations and objects.

The tensions and connections across his images operate as a conscious remixing of musical memories and sensations, from clubs to choirs, Detroit techno to music technology. Tillmans has a refreshingly non-ironic appreciation of his subjects that allows moments of beauty and intrigue to playfully unfold. He is a sensualist and recalls the body's subtle receptiveness in his pictures that are indicative of a voracious and highly cultivated visual appetite.

/ His abstractions have an almost psychedelic sense of euphoria that is musical in its transformative intensity, recalling the kinds of new aesthetics developed in contemporary electronic and dance music by artists such as Derrick May, Aphex Twin and Ritchie Hawtin. Tillmans' photographs allow numerous cross-fertilisations and moments of contemplation to open up in a way that parallels the use of music as a soundtrack to life. Rhythm, sound and melody mirror our physical and mental states and allow us to feel enhanced and unsentimentally grateful for our time. Similarly, Tillmans remixes painting languages and the spirit of music in his photographs, allowing a protean aesthetic to take hold of us as viewers and make the world both extraordinary and enthralling.

GAVIN TURK

Pop
1993

Gavin Turk's *Pop* is a life-size sculptural self-portrait with multiple layers of pop references. Turk depicts himself dressed as Sid Vicious performing Frank Sinatra's song *My Way*, while imitating a famous Elvis gunslinger image memorialised by Andy Warhol, and later re-used in Julian Temple's film *The Great Rock 'n' Roll Swindle*, which was released one year after Sid's death from a drug overdose in 1979. This sculpture is the epitome of a remix, both plundering and playful. There is a childlike dressing-up quality to it that evokes the common karaoke fantasy of acting out an identification with rebellious or glamorous pop stars. It presents the image of artist and pop star as an embalmed museum icon, made safe and consumable as just another moment frozen in history that nullifies the original pleasurably shocking effect of the young Presley and Vicious. *Pop* operates as a wry play on the reduction and commodification of cultural memory and youthful rebellion.

Pop effects a tripling of identity by mixing pop personas and that of the artist: Elvis to Sid Vicious to Turk and back again. It's a circular movement that never leaves pop moribund as it recycles well-known tropes to promote and renew itself by trading off cultural amnesia and heartfelt nostalgia. The bad boy image – the outsider with sexual aggression and energy – is a perennial favourite of popstars. It uses traditional male role models for representing and expressing strong feelings of sexuality, inadequacy, anger and ambition. These images have a particularly powerful appeal for teenagers as pop offers a soundtrack to an unsettling period of change where they experiment with personas and responsibilties. It also helps create an imaginative, creative world clearly separated from that of their parents. Pop music allows free reign for enjoyment and escapist irresponsibility to explore identity and aesthetics, which would seem to be an irresistible paradigm for the work of many contemporary artists.

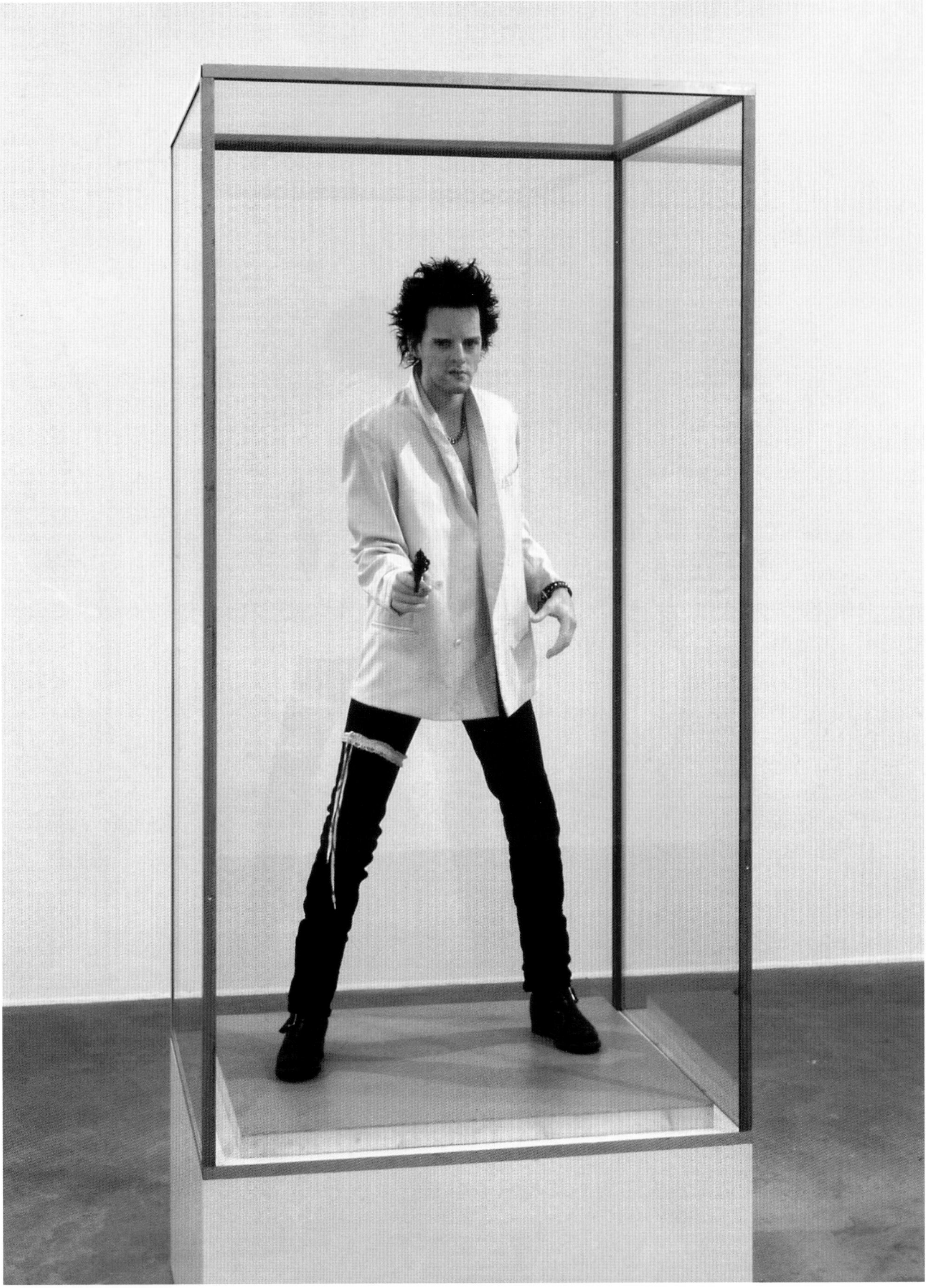

GILLIAN WEARING

01 Slight Reprise
1995

Gillian Wearing's *Slight Reprise* is a video of performances by air guitarists. It has a diaristic quality where the performers are, thankfully, non-ironic – you have to take yourself, and your music, very seriously if you are to be a competent air guitarist. The trick in playing good air guitar is the authenticity of hand and finger movements, but also, crucially, facial expression. The closed eyes, the screwed up face, the ecstatic grimace, can all be employed to give the impression of an emotionally charged rendition. We've all been to concerts or watched footage of performers going through the highly sexual motions of a guitar solo, and the cliché it embodies doesn't seem to diminish its power as a source of artistic expression. The air guitar phenomenon is all about projection and empathy with performers, wishing ourselves in their place and getting further into the music by thrashing out power chords or playing overwrought pyrotechnic solos. What true music fan hasn't done this in the privacy of their own bedroom? Wearing's piece is a portrait of fandom and the passionate love of music, but also of wish fulfilment and adult play.

01

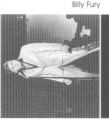

Billy Fury

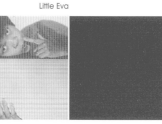

Little Eva

Switch on your TV in the twenty-first century and flip through the available stations, and it won't be long before you come across a music video being played somewhere, either individually or on a designated music video channel. Music videos are right here, right now and strangely feel like they always have been…but of course, they haven't.

Before MTV started broadcasting music videos 24 hours a day in 1981, the use of a music track combined with a visual image had been a mainstay of TV formatting, often used as 'fillers' between programmes and even on occasion as the programme's content. Prior to the introduction of video as the format for capturing the images, these short movies were shot on cine and known as 'promo films'. In the heady days of pop's 'classical' period (1958 to the early 70s), promo films were often sent out free of charge to TV stations to plug a band's latest single. Many would end up on cinema screens as fillers between the Pearl & Dean adverts and the main feature. Some bands such as The Beatles and The Rolling Stones, who had more or less given up performing live in the late 1960s, would use promos as publicity devices rather than go on the road to promote their latest product. But even the promo film had an antecedent, one which

were produced between 1940 and 1947. These three-minute 'featurettes' covered the entire spectrum of popular music and entertainment from Jazz and Blues to Country and Western, crooners to cornball comedy, even gymnasts and swimmers. One of the only two known pieces of film footage of Jazz legend Charlie Parker is a soundie, showing Parker miming to *Billie's Bounce*.

THE
UNDER-ASSISTANT
WEST
COAST
PROMO MAN

Rock 'n' roll didn't spring fully-formed from the loins of Alan Freed, Colonel Tom Parker, or anybody else for that matter. It was a long and difficult birth, bloody and snarling; the infant was clothed in black leather and sent on the road until it lost its milk teeth. Television as a medium was unable to cope with the antics of this new found fledging – left, as it were, in a basket on the steps of the TV studio.

Rock was swallowed into the world of pop and the performers were emasculated and marginalised. Viewers were most likely to see the latest teen sensation on a variety show,

Do The Locomotion (1962) or The Hollies walking down a street and singing *Look Through Any Window* (1965) as they, – yes, you've guessed it – looked through windows! But the times they were a-changin'.

WATCH THE PARKING METERS!

/ Bob Dylan's *Subterranean Homesick Blues* is often cited by cultural historians as changing the way things were done. The now legendary sequence where Dylan stands silently in an alley by the side of London's Mayfair Hotel and reels off an armful of cue cards on which the song's lyrics are drawn has been parodied, copied and paid homage to time and again over the last thirty-five years, all the way from INXS to Ever Ready batteries. The sequence was shot for two reasons. One was its inclusion in DA Pennebaker's documentary of Dylan's 1965 tour of England *Don't Look Back*. The other use, more importantly, was as a promo film.

'I'm sure that Albert [Grossman, Dylan's manager] explained to him that the deal was to pick up some footage they could use for commercials abroad. Everybody –

The Hollies

Bob Dylan

dates back to 1940 and the son of the American President.

SOUNDIES

/ The Mills Novelty Company of Chicago announced in 1940 that they were to shortly introduce a 'visual jukebox' called the Panoram. These were similar to conventional jukeboxes but had a small screen fitted inside them. After putting your nickel in the machine you could choose from a list of artists and songs. By the use of a series of mirrors and a back projection process, you could watch the song being performed right before your eyes!

/ Franklin D Roosevelt's son, James, who fronted Globe Productions – a company set up to make short films – announced that they would be supplying the product for the Mills' new invention. Their material was duly handled by the Soundies Distribution Company. The nickname 'soundies' caught on and by the middle of the Second World War the Mills-manufactured Panoram was to be found in bars and roadhouses across the United States. Despite being hampered by a long-running strike of the American Federation of Musicians, a backlash from the cinema projectionist's union, and the Second World War, over 1800 soundies

sandwiched between a comedian and a performing seal act. A few shows like *Shindig* in the USA, and *Oh Boy!* in the UK, tried to redress the balance and fill a whole time slot with music acts, but generally speaking TV was too much of a mum and dad's medium – conventional and middle class, straight and boring. Outside of the realm of mainstream television though, promos – or more correctly, promotional films – were made for public consumption, though not a great many. Most promo films were usually musical numbers simply taken from a feature film. This was the fate of Billy Fury's *Play It Cool* (1962). In France meanwhile, the concept of soundies had been revived by the Scopietone Company who quickly filled their 'visual jukeboxes' with product by artists such as Johnny Halliday and Vince Taylor. Apart from Scopietone, the outlets for these short musical features in the 1960s were as stated previously – fillers on TV shows, and as stopgaps in the cinema.

/ The format for the genre was fairly simple – feature the group or the singer miming to their latest record. If the setting could be exotic or unusual so much the better. This led creative directors to such visual heights as standing Little Eva next to a stationary steam engine for

The Kinks　The Who

The Beatles　The Rolling Stones

Queen　Genesis

The Beatles, The Stones – they did these TV promo things for free. That was standard. That was what you did on English TV at that time to sell a record.' DA Pennebaker

/ Just over a year later the footage was released to British TV companies. Though too late to help promote the single, its effect was dramatic. It made other performers aware of how unhip they looked standing around and miming. And so the slow change into the modern music video began....

LOOKING THROUGH A DEAD DOG'S EYE

/ Suddenly every band in the land was producing wacky/thoughtful/narrative-driven/meaningless promos: The Kink's *Dead End Street* (1966), banned by the BBC, The Who's *Happy Jack* (1966), The Beatles' *Strawberry Fields Forever/Penny Lane* (1967), and so it went throughout the 1960s and into the 70s. The problem was that once you'd seen these things, if they hadn't been banned like The Rolling Stones' *We Love You* (1967), that was it – once broadcast, they were gone forever. It was

important than listening to it, as radio audience figures nosedived when MTV went on air in the USA in 1981. Record companies quickly put great store into producing rock videos that would become 'a hit with the kids'. Getting a slot on MTV became an important way of guaranteeing success. Bands could now be 'broken' to the public through the medium of TV without ever setting foot inside a tour bus or wrecking a hotel room. Established acts could command a hefty budget from their record labels but younger up-and-coming bands felt they were being pushed aside in the scramble for ratings.

/ This period saw creative leaps of the imagination being ushered onto people's TV screens via the medium of the rock video. It was no surprise that a polymath artist such as David Bowie was able to use new video techniques to enhance the qualities of a song like *Ashes To Ashes* (1980). In the video, directed by David Mallet, the emphatic use of non-narrative montage, coupled with heavy dollops of surrealism, enriched Bowie's 'performer as cipher' image. In 1983, Michael Jackson hired film director John Landis (*The Blues Brothers*, *An American Werewolf In London*) to direct the promotional video for *Thriller*.

A new generation of artist/directors skilfully created a sophisticated yet highly individualistic genre of the 'short-form' visual format, crossing over easily between advertising and the music promo (a path that in several careers has led to feature film production). Jonathan Glazer's work with Radiohead, Massive Attack, Blur and Richard Ashcroft, went hand in hand with shooting ads for Guinness and Levi's, and then into his first full-length movie *Sexy Beast* (2000). Idiosyncratic American director Spike Jonze directed the highly acclaimed *Being John Malkovich* (1999) as well as directing promos for Björk, The Chemical Brothers, and the now legendary Fat Boy Slim outing *Praise You* (1999).

/ From the jook-joints of wartime America, the Soundies became the promos that begat the music videos that have now become a recognised art form. What of the future? The possibilities offered by interactive DVDs are startling and far-reaching. The viewer has the capability to remix not only the music but the images as well. The future is right here right now!

Buggles   David Bowie

Michael Jackson

Radiohead

The long-form version of this highly successful 'featurette', entitled *The Making of Michael Jackson's Thriller* (1983), became the best-selling music video spin-off to date. The concept of *Thriller* was a 'movie within a movie' and it draws heavily on Landis's reputation as a master of the horror genre. Of course the irony implicit in the whole enterprise is that it was shot on celluloid not video, a tradition still followed by many of today's performers and directors.

THIS
IS
THE
END

/ Pop is by its nature disposable, but music videos gained an enormous amount of credibility when the Museum of Modern Art in New York began collecting them in 1985. In terms of what rock had always stood for perhaps this was the death knell of the format, once rebellious and ground-breaking, even if at times cloyingly embarrassing. To be swept into the bosom of the Establishment would have once been the ultimate insult. Now it's the ultimate accolade.

/ During the 1990s the music video reached a peak of artistic credibility and success.

increasing advances in the technology of video recording that brought about the sea change in the public perception and appreciation of, what was now to be known as, the music video.

CUE
CAMERA
AND...:
BOOGIE!

/ The release of Bruce Gowers' and John Roseman's video of Queen's *Bohemian Rhapsody* (1975) heralded the dawn of a new era. With its (for the time) startling visual effects, Mercury's manqué pulp opera coincided with the growth of domestic video player ownership. Music videos could now be produced a lot more cheaply and could get a much wider distribution than their predecessors. Other artists quickly learned the lessons of using video for marketing their music. Gowers followed up his success with Queen by producing material for Genesis such as *Robbery, Assault & Battery* (1976). Former 10cc members Godley and Creme turned their talents to video production, and in 1979 Buggles prophetically proclaimed that *Video Killed The Radio Star*.

/ It quickly became apparent that 'watching' music was becoming more

01

01 —
Window Licker
by Aphex Twin
Director —
Chris Cunningham
1999

02

02

02 —
Since I left you
by The Avalanches
Director —
Leigh Marling
and Rob Leigh
2001

03 —
Dead Weight
by Beck,
Director —
Michel Gondry
1997

04

04 —
Devil's Haircut
by Beck
Director —
Mark Romanek
1996

03

05

05

05 —
All is Full of Love
by Björk
Director —
Chris Cunningham
1999

06

06

06 —
Put Your Hands Where My Eyes Can See
by Busta Rhymes
Director —
Hype Williams
1997

07

07 —
Losing My Favourite Game
by The Cardigans
Director —
Jonas Akerlund
1998

...it's some kind of ritual.

Nice shoes.

So one day she left.

08

08

08 —
Days Go By
by Dirty Vegas
Director —
Leigh Marling and
Rob Legatt
2001

09 –
I Need Love
by Elton John
Director –
Sam Taylor Wood
2001

10 –
Clint Eastwood
by the Gorillaz
Director –
Jamie Hewlet
2001

11 –
Weapon of Choice
by Fatboy Slim
Director –
Spike Jonze
2001

12 –
Praise You
by Fatboy Slim
Director –
Spike Jonze
1999

13 –
Virtual Insanity
by Jamiroquai
Director –
Jonathan Glazer
1996

14 –
Home and Dry
by The Petshop Boys
Director –
Wolfgang Tilmans
2002

15 –
Common People
by Pulp,
Director –
Hype Williams
1995

16 –
Rock DJ
by Robbie Williams
Director –
Vaughan Arnell
2000

DOUG AITKEN

Lives and works
• Los Angeles

Selected solo shows
2002
• Louisiana Museum,
Humlebaek, Denmark
• Tokyo Opera City, Tokyo

2001
• Serpentine Gallery, London
• Kunst-Werke, Berlin

2000
• Wiener Secession, Vienna

Selected group shows

2001
• Form Follows Fiction,
Castello di Rivoli, Museo d'Arte
Contemporanea, Turin

2000
• Flight Patterns,
Museum of Contemporary Art,
Los Angeles
• Whitney Biennial, Whitney
Museum of American Art,
New York
• Hypermental: Rampant
Reality 1950-2000 from
Salvador Dali to Jeff Koons,
Kunsthaus, Zurich;
Deichtorhallen, Hamburg
• Let's Entertain:
Life's Guilty Pleasures,
Walker Art Center,
Minneapolis; Centre Georges
Pompidou, Paris; Kunstmuseum
Wolfsburg, Wolfsburg,
Germany

Selected publications
2001
• Doug Aitken, Phaidon Press,
London
• Notes for New Religion.
Notes for No Religion,
Kunstmuseum Wolfsburg
and Hatje Cantz, Ostfildern,
Germany (exh cat)

2000
• I AM A BULLET,
Random House, Diamond Sea
and Bookworks, London

1998
• Metallic Sleep,
Taka Ishii Gallery, Tokyo
(exh cat)

Top ten albums +
one cassette
• The Boredoms:
Super Go Go Go!!!!!
• Carl Nillson:
Symphony No. 5
• J.S. Bach:
Glenn Gould –
The Well Tempered Clavier 2
• Steve Roden:
Eames Splint
• Yoko Ono:
Approximately Infinite Universe
• Can:
Tago Mago
• Motörhead:
Overkill
• The Stooges:
Fun House
• David Bowie:
Low
• The Carter Family:
a tape a friend made
• Brian Eno:
Here Come The Warm Jets

FIONA BANNER

Lives and works
• London

Selected solo shows
2002
• My Plinth is Your Lap,
Neuer Aachener Kunstverein,
Aachen, Germany and
Dundee Contemporary Arts,
Dundee

2001
• ARSEWOMAN,
Galerie Barbara Thumm, Berlin

1999
• Don't Look Back,
Brooke Alexander, New York

1998
• 1301PE, Los Angeles

1994
• Pushing Back The Edge
Of The Envelope, City Racing,
London

Selected publications
2002
• Fiona Banner,
Neuer Aachener Kunstverein
Aachen, Germany and
Dundee Contemporary Arts,
Dundee, Revolver, Germany
(exh cat)

1999
• Fiona Banner, 36 Full Stops,
Imprint 93, London

1998
• Esche, Charles and Lewis,
Mark, A Journal of Art,
Context and Enquiry,
Saint Martin's College of Art
& Design, London

1997
• Fiona Banner, THE NAM,
Frith Street Books/Arts Council
of England
• Fiona Banner,
Jochen Poetter, Staatliche
Kunsthalle Baden-Baden,
Baden-Baden (exh cat)

Top ten favourite albums
I don't own
• Art is the Art:
Art Pepper
• Bob Dylan:
Almost went to see Elvis,
bootleg
• Rod Mc Kewen:
Sold Out
• Art Ensemble of Chicago:
Dreaming of the Master Suite
• Bob Dylan:
Nocked Out Loaded
• Patti Smith:
Peace and Noise
• The Velvet Underground:
Live at The Boston Tea Party
• Sneakster:
Pseud Noveau
• Augustus Pablo:
Blowing with the Wind
• Kaleidoscope:
Infinite Colours Infinite Patterns

JULIE BECKER

Lives and works
• Los Angeles

Selected solo shows
2001
• In Sync: Cinema and Sound
in the work of Julie Becker
and Christian Marclay,
Whitney Museum of American
Art, New York

1997
• Kunsthalle Zurich, Zurich

Selected group shows
1999
• Peace, Museum für
Gegenwartskunst, Zurich
• Cinema Cinema -
Contemporary Art and
the Cinematic Experience,
Van Abbemuseum, Eindhoven

1997
• Model Terrains,
Carnegie Museum of Art,
Pittsburgh
• Stills: Emerging Photography
in the 1990s, Walker Art
Center, Minneapolis

1996
• 23rd Bienal de São Paolo,
São Paolo

Selected publications
2000
• Müller, Markus, 'Julie Becker:
The Invisible is Real
(Walter De Maria)', Afterall,
Issue 2
• Wollen, Peter, 'Julie Becker',
Afterall, Issue 2

1999
• de Mol, Paul, 'Cinema
Cinema in Van Abbemuseum',
Brabant Cultureel, Vol. 48,
No. 1/2, Jan/Feb

1998
• Hauptman, Jodi,
Imagining Cities -
Julie Becker's Metropolitan
Labyrinths, Fernand Léger,
Museum of Modern Art, New
York (exh cat)

1997
• Julie Becker: Researchers,
Residents, a Place to Rest,
interview with Bernhard Bürgi,
Kunsthalle Zurich, Zurich
(exh cat)

ANDREA BOWERS

Lives and works
• Los Angeles

Selected solo shows
2002
• Goldman Tevis,
Los Angeles
• Wandwinkel, Chouakri
Brahms, Berlin

2001
• Basel Statements, Art 32,
Basel

2000
• Intimate Strangers,
Sara Meltzer Gallery, New York
• Institute of Visual Arts,
University of Wisconsin,
Milwaukee

Selected group shows
2002
• L.A. On My Mind, Museum
of Contemporary Art,
Los Angeles
• Retake, Neuer Aachener
Kunstverein, Aachen, Germany
• Everybody Now, Bertha &
Karl Leubsdorf Gallery, Hunter
College, New York

2000
• Subject Plural,
Contemporary Arts Museum,
Houston
• Making Time: Considering
Time as a Material in
Contemporary Film and
Video, Palm Beach Institute of
Contemporary Art,
Palm Beach, Florida;
UCLA Hammer Museum,
University of California,
Los Angeles

Selected publications
2001
• Retake, Neuer Aachener
Kunstverein, Aachen, Germany
(exh cat)
• Everybody Now, Bertha &
Karl Leubsdorf Art Gallery,
Hunter College, New York
(exh cat)
• Siegel, Katy, 'First Take',
Artforum, January

2000
• Subject Plural,
Crowds in Contemporary Art,
Contemporary Arts Museum,
Houston (exh cat)
• Making Time: Considering
Time as a Material in
Contemporary Video and
Film, Palm Beach Institute of
Contemporary Art,
Palm Beach, Florida (exh cat)

Top ten albums
• Patti Smith:
Gone Again
• Yoko Ono:
Approximately Infinite Universe
• Janis Joplin:
Cheap Thrills
• Billie Holiday:
Lady Sings the Blues
• The Slits:
Cut
• Bessie Smith:
After You're Gone
• Royal Trux:
Cats and Dogs
• The Velvet Underground
and Nico:
The Velvet Underground
and Nico
• Nirvana:
In Utero
• Bruce Springsteen:
Nebraska

CANDICE BREITZ

Lives and works
• New York and Berlin

Selected solo shows
2001
• De Appel Foundation,
Amsterdam; Galerie Art +
Public, Geneva
• Galerie Johnen & Schöttle,
Cologne

2000
• Centre d'Art Contemporain,
Geneva
• New Museum of
Contemporary Art, New York

Selected group shows
2002
• Tele[Visions], Kunsthalle Wien,
Vienna

2001
• Looking at You, Museum
Fridericianum, Kassel
• Su La Testa!, Palazzo Delle
Papesse, Siena
• Monet's Legacy.
Series: Order and Obsession,
Hamburger Kunsthalle,
Hamburg

1999
• The Passion and the Wave,
6th International Istanbul
Biennial, Istanbul

Selected publications
2001
• Altstatt, Rosanne. 'Killing
Me Softly; An Interview with
Candice Breitz', Kunst-Bulletin,
June
• Candice Breitz: CUTTINGS,
O.K. Center for Contemporary
Art, Linz (exh cat)

2000
• Hunt, David. 'Candice Breitz:
Fighting Words', Flash Art,
March – April

1999
• Dziewior, Yilmaz. 'Candice
Breitz: Galerie Johnen &
Schöttle', Artforum, March
• Louis, Eleonora. 'Candice
Breitz: Cuttings', Springerin,
No. 3/01, Vienna

Top ten albums
• Grace Jones:
Warm Leatherette
• Kraftwerk:
The Man-Machine
• Salt'n'Pepa:
Very Necessary
• Eminem:
The Marshall Mathers LP
• Bikini Kill:
Reject All American
• Hildegard Knef:
Für mich soll's rote Rosen
regnen
• Aphex Twin:
Ventolin
• Balanescu Quartet:
Possessed
• Suzi Quatro:
If You Knew Suzi
• Peter Licht:
Sonnendeck

ANGELA BULLOCH

Lives and works
∘ London, Berlin and Vienna

Selected solo shows
2001
∘ *Z Point*, Kunsthaus Glarus, Glarus, Switzerland

2000
∘ *From the Eiffel Tower to the Riesenrad*, Galerie Kerstin Engholm, Vienna
∘ *BLOW_UP T.V.*, Schipper & Krome, Berlin
∘ *Prototypes* Galerie Hauser & Wirth & Presenhuber, Zurich

1998
∘ *Superstructure*, Museum für Gegenwartskunst, Zurich

Selected group shows
2002
∘ *Claude Monet up to Digital impressionism*, Foundation Beyeler, Basel
∘ *Frequencies [Hz] Audiovisuelle Räume*, Schirn Kunsthalle, Frankfurt

2001
∘ *Connivence*, Biennale de Lyon, Lyon

2000
∘ *EIN/Räumen. Arbeiten im Museum*, Hamburger Kunsthalle, Hamburg

Selected publications
2001
∘ *Pixel Book. Angela Bulloch*, Kunsthaus Glarus, Glarus, Switzerland

2000
∘ *Rule Book. Angela Bulloch*, Stefan Kalmär (ed.), Bookworks, London

1998
∘ *Satellite*, Stefan Kalmär and Angela Bulloch (eds.), Museum für Gegenwartskunst, Zurich and Le Consortium, Dijon

1994
∘ *Angela Bulloch*, CCC Tours; FRAC-Languedoc Roussillon, Kunstverein Hamburg, Hamburg

DEXTER DALWOOD

Lives and works
∘ London

Selected solo shows
2002
∘ *Dexter Dalwood: New Paintings*, Gagosian Gallery, Los Angeles

2000
∘ *Dexter Dalwood: New Paintings*, Gagosian Gallery, London

1995
∘ Galerie Unwahr, Berlin

1992
∘ Clove Building, London

Selected group shows
2002
∘ *View Five: Westworld*, Mary Boone Gallery, New York

2001
∘ *Twisted: Urban and Visionary Landscapes in Contemporary Painting*, Van Abbemuseum, Eindhoven

1999
∘ *Caught*, 303 Gallery, New York
∘ *Neurotic Realism: Part Two*, Saatchi Gallery, London

1998
∘ *Die Young Stay Pretty*, Institute of Contemporary Art, London

Selected publications
2001
∘ *Twisted: Urban and Visionary Landscapes in Contemporary Painting*, Van Abbemuseum, Eindhoven (exh cat)

2000
∘ *Dexter Dalwood: New Paintings*, Gagosian Gallery, London (exh cat)

1998
∘ *Die Young Stay Pretty*, Institute of Contemporary Art, London (exh cat)
∘ *The New Neurotic Realism*, Saatchi Gallery, London (exh cat)

Top ten albums
∘ Cloudhead: *Cloudhead*
∘ Prince and the Revolution: *Purple Rain*
∘ Captain Beefheart: *Safe as Milk*
∘ The Velvet Underground and Nico: *The Velvet Underground and Nico*
∘ The Fall: *Infotainment Scan*
∘ The Rolling Stones: *Exile on Mainstreet*
∘ Tim Buckley: *Greetings from L.A.*
∘ The Aphex Twin: *Classics*
∘ The Clash: *The Clash*
∘ Barry Adamson: *Oedipus Schmoedipus*

RINEKE DIJKSTRA

Lives and works
∘ Amsterdam

Selected solo shows
2001
∘ *Israel Portraits*, Herzliya Museum of Art, Herzliya, Israel
∘ *Focus: Rineke Dijkstra*, Art Institute of Chicago, Chicago

2000
∘ *Rineke Dijkstra*, Anthony d'Offay Gallery, London

1999
∘ *Portraits*, DAAD Galerie, Berlin

1997
∘ *Location*, The Photographers' Gallery, London

Selected group shows
2001
∘ *49th Venice Biennale*, Venice

2000
∘ *Eurovision*, Saatchi Gallery, London
∘ *Let's Entertain*, Walker Art Center, Minneapolis; Centre Georges Pompidou, Paris; Kunstmuseum Wolfsburg, Wolfsburg, Germany

1999
∘ *Citibank Private Bank Photography Prize*, Photographers' Gallery, London
∘ *Modern Starts: People, Places, Things*, Museum of Modern Art, New York

1998
∘ *The Global City*, Gemeentemuseum Helmond, The Netherlands

Selected publications
2001
∘ *Rineke Dijkstra Portraits*, Institute of Contemporary Art, Boston and Hatje Cantz, Ostifildern, Germany (exh cat)

1998
∘ *Rineke Dijkstra: Menschenbilder*, Museum Folkwang, Essen (exh cat)
∘ *Rineke Dijkstra: The Buzz Club, Liverpool: Mysteryworld, Zaandam, The Netherlands 1996-1997*, Sprengel Museum, Hanover (exh cat)

1997
∘ *Location*, Photographers' Gallery, London (exh cat)
∘ *Rineke Dijkstra: Beaches*, Codax Publishing, Zurich

Top ten
∘ Hotel Costes: *Hotel Costes*
∘ Faithless: *Back to Mine*
∘ Fatboy Slim: *Half Between the Gutter and the Stars*
∘ Madonna: *Ray of Light*
∘ Costes: *La Suite*
∘ Groove Armada: *Vertigo*
∘ ir: *Premieres Symptones*
∘ Danny Tenglia: *Global Underground*
∘ Thievery Corporation: *The Mirror Conspiracy*
∘ Kruder and Dorfmeister: *The K & D Sessions*

RODNEY GRAHAM

Lives and works
∘ Vancouver

Selected solo shows
2002
∘ Madison Art Center, Madison, Wisconsin

2001
∘ Hamburger Bahnhof, Berlin

2000
∘ Kunstverein München, Munich

1999
∘ Kunsthalle Wien, Vienna

1998
∘ Wexner Center for the Arts, Columbus, Ohio

Selected group shows
2002
∘ *13th Sydney Biennial*, Sydney
∘ *Rock My World*, California College of Arts and Crafts, San Francisco
∘ *Govett-Brewster Art Gallery*, New Plymouth, New Zealand

2001
∘ *Neue Welt*, Frankfurter Kunstverein, Frankfurt
∘ *Wiederaufnahme*, Neuer Aachener Kunstverein, Aachen, Germany

Selected publications
1998
∘ *Vexation Island and Other Works*, Art Gallery of York University, Toronto (exh cat)

1997
∘ *Island Thought. An Archipelagic Journal Published at Irregular Intervals*, 49th Venice Biennale (exh cat)

1994
∘ *Rodney Graham: Works from 1976 to 1994*, Art Gallery of York University, Toronto (exh cat)

1990
∘ *Rodney Graham: Parsifal*, Galerie Johnen & Schöttle, Cologne (exh cat)

1988
∘ *Rodney Graham*, Vancouver Art Gallery, Vancouver (exh cat)

Top Ten Songs
∘ The Only Ones: *Big Sleep*
∘ Cass Elliot: *Jesus Was a Crossmaker*
∘ Paul Williams: *Someday Man*
∘ The Evaporators: *I Don't Need My Friends (To Tell Me Who My Friends Are)*
∘ St. Etienne: *Join Our Club*
∘ Glenn Campbell: *Marie*
∘ The Ronettes: *Wish I Never Saw The Sunshine*
∘ Vancouver Nights: *Joy Is Like The Rain*
∘ Left Bank: *My Friend Today*
∘ Love: *Orange Skies*

ANDREAS GURSKY

Lives and works
∘ Düsseldorf

Selected solo shows
2001
∘ Museum of Modern Art, New York; Museo Nacional Centro de Arte Reina Sofia, Madrid; Centre Georges Pompidou, Paris

1999
∘ Castello di Rivoli, Museo d'Arte Contemporanea, Turin; Centro Cultural de Belém, Lisbon

1998
∘ *Andreas Gursky: Fotografien 1984-1998*, Kunstmuseum Wolfsburg, Wolfsburg; Fotomuseum Winterthur; Kunsthalle Düsseldorf, Düsseldorf

1997
∘ *Currents 27: Andreas Gursky*, Milwaukee Art Museum, Milwaukee; Henry Art Gallery at the University of Washington, Seattle; Contemporary Arts Museum, Houston

1994
∘ *Andreas Gursky: Fotografien 1984-1993*, Deichtorhallen, Hamburg; De Appel Foundation, Amsterdam; Le Case d'Arte, Milano

Selected group shows
2001
∘ *German Festival in India*, Karnataka Chitrakala Parishath, Bangalore and National Gallery of Modern Art, New Delhi
∘ *Museum as Subjects*, National Museum of Art, Osaka

2000
∘ *Walker Evans & Company*, Museum of Modern Art, New York
∘ *An Expanded View: Recent Acquisitions: Photography*, Solomon R. Guggenheim Museum, New York
∘ *Große Illusionen: Thomas Demand, Andreas Gursky, Edward Ruscha*, Kunstmuseum Bonn, Germany; Museum of Contemporary Art, North Miami, Florida

Selected publications
2001
∘ *Andreas Gursky*, Museum of Modern Art, New York (exh cat)

1998
∘ *Andreas Gursky: Fotografie von 1984 bis heute*, Kunsthalle Düsseldorf, Düsseldorf (exh cat)
∘ *Andreas Gursky: Fotografien 1984-1998*, Kunstmuseum Wolfsburg, Wolfsburg (exh cat)

1995
∘ *Andreas Gursky: Montparnasse*, Portikus, Frankfurt (exh cat)

Ten favourite albums
∘ Klaus Föttinger: *Sunset Boulevard*
∘ Westbam: *We Never Stop Living*
∘ Sven Väth: *Genetic Architecture*
∘ Alcazar: *Casino*
∘ Reinhard Vogt: *In reiner Freundschaft*
∘ Kreidler: *Wonder*
∘ Thomas Brinkmann: *Jutta*
∘ Captain Beefheart and the Magic Band: *Shiny Beast*
∘ Window Licker: *Nannu*
∘ Antonelli: *Time Destroying Machine*

GARY HUME

Lives and works
• London

Selected solo shows
2001
• *Gary Hume*,
Matthew Marks Gallery,
New York

1999
• *Gary Hume*, Dean Gallery,
National Galleries of Scotland,
Edinburgh
• *Gary Hume*, British Pavilion,
48th Venice Biennale, Venice

1996
• *Gary Hume*,
23rd Bienal de São Paolo,
São Paolo

1995
• *Gary Hume*,
Jay Jopling/White Cube,
London

Selected group shows
2001
• *Beautiful Productions.
Art to play, art to wear, art to
own*, Whitechapel, London
• *Public Offerings*,
Museum of Contemporary
Arts, Los Angeles

2000
• *Out There*, White Cube²,
London

1997
• *Sensation*,
Royal Academy of Arts,
London

1988
• *Ian Davenport, Gary Hume,
Michael Landy*, Karsten
Schubert Ltd, London
• *Freeze, Part II*,
Surrey Docks, London

MARK LECKEY

Lives and works
• London

Selected solo shows
2002
• *Dubplate*,
Gavin Brown's enterprise,
New York

2000
• *London: My Part in its
Downfall*, Galerie Buchholz,
Cologne

Selected group shows
2002
• *Hotel Sub Rosa*,
Cabinet@Marc Foxx,
Los Angeles

2001
• *Sound & Vision*, Institute
of Contemporary Art, London

2000
• *Village Disco*, Cabinet,
London
• *Century City*, Tate Modern,
London

1999
• *Crash*, Institute of
Contemporary Art, London

Selected publications
2002
• Higgs, Matthew,
'Openings', *Artforum*, April

2001
• La Frenier, Steve,
'Mark Leckey', *Index*,
September
• Mellors, Nathaniel,
'Revolutions Per Second',
Frieze, October

Top ten favourite albums
of the last four years
• Mission FM:
Heartless Crew
• Crass:
Stations of the Cross
• *Reggae Hits Vol. 23*
• Various:
*Speed Limit 140 BPM
Plus Eight*
• Donateller:
Radiohead
• Roxy Music:
Roxy Music
• The Shangri Las:
Golden Hits of the Shangri Las
• Hair:
Original Cast Recording
• Energy Flash:
'Ardcore compilation
• Todd Edwards:
Prima Edizone

DAWN MELLOR

Lives and works
• London

Selected solo shows
2002
• *Dawn Mellor*,
Team Gallery, New York

2001
• *Madame X and the
Party Tricks*, Victoria Miro
Gallery, London

2000
• *Me & Mrs Jones*, Galleria II
Capricorna, Venice
• *The Baby Doll Murders*,
Galerie Drantmann, Brussels
• *Wishing I was someone
else instead*, Victoria Miro
Gallery, London

Selected group shows
2001
• *Works on Paper:
From Acconci to Zittel*, Victoria
Miro Gallery, London

1998
• *London Now*,
Saks Fifth Avenue, New York
• *Alice*, Cornerhouse,
Manchester
• *Motherhood*, City Racing,
London

1997
• *Likeness*, Manchester City
Art Galleries, Manchester

Top ten albums
• Marianne Faithful:
Broken English
• Hole:
Live Through This
• Gina X:
No GDM
• The Slits:
Cut
• Janis Joplin:
Pearl
• Nina Hagen:
Nun sex monk rock
• Judy Garland:
*Judy Garland at
Carnegie Hall*
• Amanda Lear:
Sweet Revenge
• Siouxsie and the Banshees:
Ju Ju
• Dusty Springfield:
Dusty in Memphis

CHRIS OFILI

Lives and Works
• London

Selected solo shows
2000
• *Chris Ofili Drawings*,
Victoria Miro Gallery, London

1999
• *Afrobiotics*, Gavin Brown's
enterprise, New York

1998-9
• *Chris Ofili*,
Southampton City Art Gallery,
Southhampton; Serpentine
Gallery, London; Whitworth Art
Gallery, Manchester

1997
• *Pimpin ain't easy but
it sure is fun*, Contemporary
Fine Art, Berlin

1996
• *Afrodizzia*,
Victoria Miro Gallery, London

Selected group shows
2001
• *Cavepainting*,
Santa Monica Museum of Art,
Santa Monica, California

1999
• *Carnegie International*,
Carnegie Museum of Art,
Pittsburgh

1998
• *The Turner Prize*,
Tate Gallery, London

1993
• *Shit Sale*, Brick Lane, London

1992-3
• *Pachipamwe
International artists' workshop*,
Bulawayo Art Gallery, Harare

Selected publication
1998
• *Chris Ofili*,
Southampton City Art Gallery,
Southampton and
Serpentine Gallery, London
(exh cat)

JULIAN OPIE

• Lives and works
London

Selected solo shows
2001
• Ikon Gallery, Birmingham

1993
• Hayward Gallery, London

1991
• Kunsthalle, Bern
• Wiener Secession, Vienna

1985
• Institute of Contemporary
Arts, London

Selected group shows
2000
• *Between cinema and a hard
place*, Tate Modern, London

1998
• *11th Sydney Biennial*, Sydney

1997
• *47th Venice Biennale*,
Venice

1993
• *43rd Venice Biennale*,
Venice

1987
• *Documenta 8*, Kassel

Selected publications
2001
• *Julian Opie*, Lisson Gallery,
London (exh cat)
• *Julian Opie*, Ikon Gallery,
Birmingham (exh cat)

1997
• *Julian Opie*, Indian
Trienniale, Delhi (exh cat)

1993
• *Julian Opie*, Hayward
Gallery, London (exh cat)

1984
• *Julian Opie*, Kölnischer
Kunstverein, Cologne (exh cat)

Top ten albums
• Bert Kaempfert:
Swinging Safari
• J.S. Bach:
Brandenburg Concertos
• Simon and Garfunkel:
Bridge over Troubled Waters
• Bob Dylan:
Nashville Skyline
• Future Sound of London:
FSOL
• William Orbit:
Strange Cargo
• Talvin Singh:
Ha
• John Barry:
The Beyondness of Things
• The Chemical Brothers:
Exit Planet Dust
• Handel:
Messiah

WOLFGANG TILLMANS

Lives and works
• London

Selected solo shows
2001
• *Aufsicht*,
Deichtorhallen, Hamburg

1998
• *Fruciones*, Espacio Uno,
Museo Reina Sofia, Madrid

1997
• *I didn't inhale*,
Chisenhale Gallery, London

1995
• Kunsthalle Zürich, Zurich

1993
• Galerie Daniel Buchholz,
Cologne

Selected group shows
2000
• *The Turner Prize*,
Tate Britain, London

1998
• *From the Corner of the Eye*,
Stedelijk Museum, Amsterdam

1997
• *Absolute Landscape*,
Yokohama Museum of Art,
Yokohama

1996
• *New Photography*,
Museum of Modern Art,
New York

1994
• *L'Hiver de l'Amour*,
Musée d'Art Moderne de la
Ville de Paris, Paris

Selected publications
2001
• *View From Above*,
Hatje Cantz, Ostfildern,
Germany

1998
• *Parkett*, No.53

1997
• *Concorde*,
Verlag der Buchhandlung
Walther König, Cologne

1996
• *for when I'm weak
I'm strong*, Kunstmuseum
Wolfsburg, Wolfsburg,
Germany (exh cat)

1995
• *Wolfgang Tillmans*, Benedikt
Taschen Verlag, Cologne

Top ten albums
• Soft Cell:
Non Stop Erotic Cabaret
• New Order:
Technique
• Billie Ray Martin:
Deadline for my Memories
• Taize Community:
Chants from Taize
• The Pet Shop Boys:
Please
• Neil Young and Crazy Horse:
Live Rust
• The Beloved:
Happiness
• Miss Kitten and The Hacker:
The First Album
• Plastikman:
Muzik
• Arvo Pärt:
Tabula Rasa

GAVIN TURK

Lives and works
• London

Selected solo shows
2001
• *More Stuff*, Centre d'Art
Contemporain, Geneva

1999
• *The Importance of Being
Ernesto*, Galerie Krinzinger,
Vienna

1998
• *The Stuff Show*,
South London Gallery, London

1996
• *Turkish*, Galerie Aurel
Scheibler, Cologne

1993
• *Collected Works 1989–93*,
Jay Jopling, London

Selected group shows
2002
• *Second Skin*,
Henry Moore Institute, Leeds

1998
• *Material Culture*,
Hayward Gallery, London

1997
• *Sensation*,
Royal Academy, London
• *Live Stock Market*,
Charlotte Road, London

1996
• *Fuck Off*, Bank, London

Selected publications
1998
• Farquarson, Alex,
*Gavin Turk Collected Works
1994-1998*, Art Data, London

1993
• *Gavin Turk Collected Works
1989-1993*, Jay Jopling,
London (exh cat)

Top ten albums
• Junior Murvin:
Police and Thieves
• Fela Ransome Kuti
and the Africa 70:
Open and Close
• RDB:
Rhythm Dhol Bass
• Orchestra Baobab:
Pirates Choice
• Jackie Mittoo:
Keyboard King at Studio One
• Art Blakey and
the Jazz Messengers:
Drum Suite
• King Jammy meets Dry
and Heavy:
In the Jaws of the Tiger
• Las Samplers:
Rhythm Digitalis
• The JBs:
Pass the Peas
• NWA:
Straight Outta Compton

ELIZABETH PEYTON

Lives and works
• Orient, New York

Selected solo shows
2002
• Neugerriemschneider,
Berlin
• Salzburger Kunstverein,
Salzburg

2001
• Gavin Brown's enterprise,
New York
• Deichtorhallen, Hamburg

2000
• Westfälischer Kunstverein,
Münster, Germany

1998
• Kunstmuseum Wolfsburg,
Wolfsburg, Germany;
Museum für Gegenwartskunst,
Basel

Selected group shows
2002
• *DEAR PAINTER, Paint Me*,
Centre Georges Pompidou,
Paris
• *Contemporary Drawing:
Eight Propositions*,
Museum of Modern Art,
New York

2001
• *Longing and Memory*,
Los Angeles County Museum
of Art, Los Angeles
• *Abbild recent
portraiture and depiction*,
Landesmuseum Joanneum,
Graz
• *About Face: Selections
from the Prints and Illustrated
Books Department*,
Museum of Modern Art,
New York

Selected publications
2001
• Peyton, Elizabeth, *Prince
Eagle*. Powerhouse Books and
Thea Westreich, New York
• Pruitt, Rob and Lafreniere,
Steve, 'Elizabeth Peyton',
Index, July

1998
• Ursprung, Philip, 'In Praise
of Hands. Elizabeth Peyton's
Painting', *Parkett*, No.53
• *Elizabeth Peyton: Craig*.
Edition Salzau and Verlag der
Buchhandlung Walter König,
Cologne

1997
• Peyton, Elizabeth,
Live Forever. Synergy, Inc.,
Tokyo

RICKY SWALLOW

Lives and works
• Melbourne

Selected solo shows
2002
• Karyn Lovegrove Gallery,
Los Angeles

2001
• *For Those Who Came in
Late, Matrix 191*, Berkeley Art
Museum, San Francisco
• *Above Ground Sculpture*,
Dunedin Public Art Gallery,
New Zealand

2000
• *Unplugged*, Darren Knight
Gallery, Sydney
• *Individual Ape*, Hot Rod Tea
Room, Oslo

Selected group shows
2001
• *Casino*, Smak Museum,
Ghent, Belgium
• *Swallow Swenson*,
Museum of Contemporary Art,
Sydney
• *Utopia/ROR*, Kiasma,
Museum of Contemporary Art,
Helsinki

2000
• *Keith Edmier,
Ricky Swallow, Erik Swenson*,
Andrea Rosen Gallery,
New York

1999
• *Signs of Life*,
Melbourne International
Biennial, Melbourne

Selected publications
2001
• Kent, Rachel, *Classical
Contemporary, Swallow
Swenson*, Museum of
Contemporary Art, Sydney
• Palmer, Daniel, 'Shadow
Play', *Frieze*, April
• Brae, Marah, 'The Voyeur
Awakes', *Art and Australia*,
April
• Paton, Justin,
*The Recreation Room, Above
Ground Sculpture*, Dunedin
Public Art Gallery, Dunedin,
New Zealand

1999
• Colless, Edward,
*The World Ends when its Parts
Wear Out*, *Memory Made
Plastic*, Artist's publication in
association with Darren Knight
Gallery, Sydney

GILLIAN WEARING

Lives and works
• London

Selected solo shows
2002
• *Mass Observation*,
Museum of Contemporary Art,
Chicago

2001
• *Sous Influence*,
Musée d'Art Moderne de la
Ville de Paris, Paris;
Fundacio la Caixa, Madrid
• Serpentine Gallery, London

1999
• Maureen Paley
Interim Art, London

Selected group shows
2002
• Bienal de São Paulo,
São Paulo
• *13th Sydney Biennal*,
Museum of Contemporary Art,
Sydney

2000
• *Quotidiana*,
Castello di Rivoli, Museo d'Arte
Contemporanea, Turin

1997
• *The Turner Prize*,
Tate Gallery, London
• *Sensation*,
Royal Academy of Arts,
London

Selected publications
2001
• *Gillian Wearing,
Sous influence*, Musée d'Art
Moderne de la Ville de Paris,
Paris (exh cat)
• *Gillian Wearing*,
Fundacio la Caixa, Madrid
(exh cat)
• *Gillian Wearing*,
Serpentine Gallery, London
(exh cat)
• *Gillian Wearing*,
Phaidon Press, London

1997
• *Signs that say what you
want them to say and not
Signs that say what someone
else wants you to say*,
Maureen Paley, Interim Art,
London (exh cat)

GARY HUME

Michael
2001
(Pg 61)
Gloss paint on aluminium
1219mm diameter
Private collection,
London

DOUG AITKEN

Hysteria
1998
(Pg 41)
Video (4 screen projection)
Dimensions variable
Courtesy Victoria Miro Gallery,
London and 303 Gallery,
New York

CANDICE BREITZ

Double Karen (Close to You)
2000
(Pg 48-49)
DVD
Size variable
Private collection, courtesy
of asprey jacques,
London

MARK LECKEY

Fiorucci Made Me Hardcore
1999
(Pg 62-63)
DVD
Size variable
Courtesy Cabinet,
London and
Gavin Brown's enterprise,
New York

CHRIS OFILI

Popcorn Shells
1996
(Pg 66)
Acrylic, oil, resin,
paper collage, map pins
and elephant dung on canvas
1830mm x 1220mm
Arts Council Collection,
Hayward Gallery,
London

FIONA BANNER

Don't Look Back
1999
(Pg 43)
3 part screen print
2600mm x 3200mm
Tate Collection

ANGELA BULLOCH

Disco Floor_Bootleg:16
2002
(Pg 51)
Pixel boxes
4000mm x 4000mm x 650mm
Magnani,
London

RINEKE DIJKSTRA

The Buzz Club, Liverpool (UK)
Mysteryworld, Zaandam (NL)
1996
(Pg 55)
DVD
Size variable
Courtesy
Anthony d'Offay Gallery,
London

DAWN MELLOR

Love on the Rocks
2001
(Pg 64)
Oil on canvas
1650mm x 1520mm
Courtesy the artist
and Victoria Miro Gallery,
London

Afrodizzia
1996
(Pg 67)
Oil paint, paper collage,
glitter, polyester resin, map pins
and elephant dung on linen
2440mm x 1830mm
The Saatchi Gallery,
London

JULIE BECKER

Suburban Legend
1999
(Pg 47)
Video installation
Size variable
Courtesy of the artist and
Greene Naftali Gallery,
New York

DEXTER DALWOOD

Ian Curtis' Bedroom
2001
(Pg 53)
Oil on canvas
2082mm x 1752mm
Private collection,
Italy

no, no, no, no, no
2001
(Pg 64)
Oil on canvas
1830mm x 1220mm
Courtesy the artist
and Victoria Miro Gallery,
London

JULIAN OPIE

Damon from Blur
2000
(Pg 68)
Vinyl on wooden stretcher
1920mm x 1520mm
Courtesy of Lisson Gallery,
London

ANDREA BOWERS

Democracy's Body -
Dance Dance Revolution
2001
(Pg 47)
4 DVDs, 4 LCD monitors,
4 audiosystems, 4 DVD players
Size variable
Courtesy of the artist and
Sara Meltzer Gallery,
New York

Neverland
(Michael Jackson's Bedroom)
1999
(Pg 52)
Oil on canvas
1830mm x 2130mm
Private collection

RODNEY GRAHAM

Phonokinetoscope
2001
(Pg 57)
16mm film
and vinyl record
Size variable
Courtesy Galerie Nelson,
Paris

Leader of the Pack
2001
(Pg 65)
Oil on canvas
1820mm x 1250mm
Courtesy the artist
and Victoria Miro Gallery,
London

engines-footsteps-voices
1999
(Pg 69)
Aluminium paint, sound system,
perspex, c-print on paper
1220mm x 1800mm x 120mm
Courtesy of Lisson Gallery,
London

Paisley Park
1998
(Pg 52)
Oil on canvas
1520mm x 1830mm
The Saatchi Gallery,
London

ANDREAS GURSKY

May Day IV
2000
(Pg 59)
C-print
2050mm x 5050mm
Courtesy the artist
and Victoria Miro Gallery,
London

RICKY SWALLOW

Upgrade and Afterlife/
Four Demonstration Models
2001

Another Model for the
Endless Excavation
2001
(Pg 72)
Record player, plastic
and Milliput
440mm x 370mm x 250mm
Private collection, Hong Kong.
Courtesy of
Darren Knight Gallery,
Sydney

WOLFGANG TILLMANS

Miss Kittin
2001
(Pg 74)
C-print
610mm x 510mm
Courtesy Maureen Paley
Interim Art,
London

outside Snax Club
2001
(Pg 72)
Ink-jet print
1950mm x 1350mm
Courtesy Maureen Paley
Interim Art,
London

ELIZABETH PEYTON

Spencer at Florent
2001
(Pg 70)
Oil on board
304mm x 228mm
Collection of Nina and
Frank Moore,
New York

Modeling the Marantz
Experiment
2001
(Pg 73)
Record player, plastic
and Milliput
230mm x 460mm x 350mm
Private collection, Hong Kong.
Courtesy of
Darren Knight Gallery,
Sydney

paper drop
2001
(Pg 74)
C-print
610mm x 510mm
Courtesy Maureen Paley
Interim Art,
London

Evan reading
at the Reading Festival
1997
(Pg 70)
Oil on board
304mm x 229mm
Private collection,
Switzerland

Model for Meticulous
Maintenance
2001
(Pg 73)
Record player, plastic
and Milliput
260mm x 490mm x 370mm
Private collection, Hong Kong.
Courtesy of
Darren Knight Gallery,
Sydney

Super Collider-A
2001
Ink-jet print
2000mm x 1370mm
Courtesy Maureen Paley
Interim Art,
London

Rhythim is Rhythim
1999
C-print
570mm x 610mm
Courtesy Maureen Paley
Interim Art,
London

GAVIN TURK

Pop
1993
(Pg 77)
Waxwork in wood, glass
and brass vitrine
2790mm x 1150mm
x 1150mm
The Saatchi Gallery,
London

Flower Liam
1996
(Pg 70)
Oil on board
430mm x 350mm
Collection Mark Fletcher
and Tobias Meyer,
New York

Mental Picture #52
2000
(Pg 75)
C-print
610mm x 510mm
Courtes Maureen Paley
Interim Art,
London

Choir (Jubilate Deo)
1993
C-print
510mm x 610mm
Courtesy Maureen Paley
Interim Art,
London

Mark
1996
Oil on board
252mm x 201mm
Laura and Stafford Braumand

Wronging the Robots
2001
(Pg 73)
Record player, plastic
and Milliput
230mm x 460mm x 350mm
Private collection, Hong Kong.
Courtesy of
Darren Knight Gallery,
Sydney

303 in grass
1993
(Pg 74)
C-print
510mm x 610mm
Courtesy Maureen Paley
Interim Art,
London

GILLIAN WEARING

Slight Reprise
1995
(Pg 79)
DVD
Size variable
Courtesy Maureen Paley
Interim Art,
London

Kurt (Sunglasses)
1995
(Pg 71)
Oil on board
4000mm x 3000mm
Collection Marcel Brient,
Paris

Podium
1999
C-print
610mm x 510mm
Courtesy Maureen Paley
Interim Art,
London

THE AVALANCHES

Since I left You
2001
Blue Source
Directed by
Leigh Marling and Rob Legatt
© XL Records Ltd.

APHEX TWIN

Windowlicker
2000
Black Dog Films
Directed by
Chris Cunningham
© Warp Records

BADLY DRAWN BOY

Disillusioned
2001
Hammer & Tongs
Directed by
Garth Jennings
© Twisted Nerve Records

BEASTIE BOYS

Sabotage
1994
Satellite Films
Directed by
Spike Jonze
© Capitol

BECK

Deadweight
1997
Partizan
Directed by
Michel Gondry
© Geffen Records

Devil's Haircut
1996
Anonymous Content
Directed by
Mark Romanek
© Geffen Records

BJÖRK

All Is Full Of Love
1999
Black Dog Films
Directed by
Chris Cunningham
© Elektra Records

Human Behaviour
1993
Partizan
Directed by
Michel Gondry
© Elektra Records

BRITNEY SPEARS

...Baby One More Time
1999
Zomba
Directed by
Nigel Dick
© Jive/Silvertone

BUSTA RHYMES

Gimme Some Mo'
1999
Big Dog Films
Directed by
Hype Williams
© Elektra Records

**Put Your Hands Where
My Eyes Can See**
1997
Big Dog Films
Directed by
Hype Williams
© Elektra Records

THE CARDIGANS

My Favourite Game
1998
Oil Factory
Directed by
Jonas Akerlund
© Stockholm Records/
Polygram

THE CHEMICAL BROTHERS

Let Forever Be
2000
Partizan
Directed by
Michel Gondry
© Freestyle Dust/Virgin

DIRTY VEGAS

Days Go By
2001
Blue Source
Directed by
Leigh Marling and Rob Legatt
© Credence/Parlophone

ELTON JOHN

I Want Love
2001
Dixie Linder and
Denny Tedesco
Directed by
Sam Taylor-Wood
© Mercury Records

EMINEM

The Real Slim Shady
2001
Geronimo Films
Directed by
Philip G. Atwell & Dr Dre
© Aftermath/Interscope
Records

Stan
2001
Aftermath/Interscape
Directed by Philip G.
Atwell & Dr Dre
© Aftermath/Interscope
Records

FATBOY SLIM

Praise You
1999
The Director's
Bureau/Satellite Films
Directed by
Roman Coppola
© Skint Records

Right Here, Right Now
2000
Hammer & Tongs
Directed by
Dominic Leung
© Skint Records

Weapon Of Choice
2001
The Director's
Bureau/Satellite Films
Directed by
Spike Jonze
© Skint Records

GORILLAZ

Clint Eastwood
2001
Passion Pictures
Directed by
Jamie Hewlett
© Parlophone, EMI

JAMIROQUAI

Virtual Insanity
1996
Academy
Directed by
Jonathan Glazer
© The Work Group/Sony

LAURYN HILL

Doo Wop (That Thing)
1998
Academy
Directed by
Big TVI
© Ruff House

MADONNA

Ray of Light
1998
Oil Factory
Directed by
Jonas Akerlund
© Warner Bros.

MANSUN

Taxloss
1997
Oil Factory
Directed by
Roman Coppola
© Parlophone, EMI

MISSY ELLIOT

The Rain
1997
Big Dog Films
Directed by
Hype Williams
© Elektra Records

NIRVANA

Smells Like Teen Spirit
1991
Straylight Productions
Directed by
Samuel Bayer
© Geffen Records

THE PET SHOP BOYS

Home and Dry
2001
Directed by
Wolfgang Tillmans
© Parlophone, EMI

PJ HARVEY

Good Fortune
2001
Oil Factory
Directed by
Sophie Muller
© Island Records Ltd.

PRODIGY

Smack My Bitch Up
1997
Oil Factory
Directed by
Jonas Akerlund
© Elektra Records

PULP

Common People
1995
Oil Factory
Directed by
Pedro Romhanyi
© Island Records Ltd.

RADIOHEAD

Karma Police
1997
Academy Commercials Ltd
Directed by
Jonathan Glazer
© Parlophone, EMI

REM

Imitation Of Life
2001
Hammer & Tongs
Directed by
Garth Jennings
© Warner Bros.

ROBBIE WILLIAMS

Rock DJ
2001
Palomar
Directed by
Vaughan Arnell
© Chrysalis

SQUAREPUSHER

Come On My Selector
1999
Big Dog Films
Directed by
Chris Cunningham
© Warp Records

SUPERGRASS

Pumpin' On Your Stereo
2000
Hammer & Tongs
Directed by
Dominic Leung
© UNI/Island Records Ltd.

MARY

Mary
1999
Oil Factory
Directed by
Sophie Muller
© UNI/Island Records Ltd.

TLC

No Scrubs
1999
Mars Media/Big Dog Films
Directed by
Hype Williams
© La Face/Arista

UNKLE

Rabbit In Your Headlights
1999
Academy Commercials Ltd
Directed by
Jonathan Glazer
© Mo Wax